Osteoarthritis

An Integrative Medicine Treatment Program

A SPECIAL REPORT FROM THE EDITORS OF

Dr. Andrew Weil's Self Healing

Self Healing is Dr. Andrew Weil's monthly health newsletter, which is published by MSX, Inc., 42 Pleasant St., Watertown MA 02472; *www.drweilselfhealing.com*; (617) 926-0200. For subscription information, please call (800) 523-3296.

ISBN 0–9706414–5–1
Printed in the United States of America

WRITER AND RESEARCHER Jessica Cerretani

MEDICAL EDITOR Andrew Weil, MD

EDITORS Cari Nierenberg | Dan Fields

EDITORIAL INTERNS Jennifer Cotie | Maggie Cramer | Heather McNally

ART DIRECTION & DESIGN Mary Lynch

PUBLISHER Janesse Thaw Bruce

CIRCULATION Shirley Barry | Devin McCloskey | Barbara Hamwey

PRODUCTION Mandy Stone-DerHagopian

Table of Contents

Introduction

Dear Reader,

Welcome to *Osteoarthritis: An Integrative Treatment Program.* If you're reading this *Self Healing* special report, it's probably because you either have osteoarthritis (OA) or know someone who does. If you have OA, I realize that you're all too familiar with stiff, swollen joints that can make even simple movements feel painful. And you're probably also concerned about taking conventional pain medications, or are hoping to delay joint surgery.

That's why the editors of *Self Healing* and I have created this special report. I'm encouraged by surveys that show the majority of people with arthritis seek out alternative therapies, supplements, and other nondrug approaches. These natural measures, when combined with conventional medication and other treatments as needed, can make a big difference in relieving joint pain, stiffness, and other symptoms. I think that OA is a great example of a condition that's best treated with a mix of the most effective conventional, alternative, and commonsense lifestyle approaches. Known as integrative medicine, this type of care aims to take advantage of the body's innate healing capacity, rather than just treating symptoms of disease. This clear, in-depth report offers a comprehensive integrative treatment program for OA.

In the next several chapters, you'll read in more detail about a wide range of therapeutic choices for OA, including the benefits and risks of these treatments, so that you can make informed decisions about what's best for your health. The therapies, supplements, and other approaches discussed in this report are the ones that are the best researched, the most popular, and the ones I'm most often asked about. As the medical editor of this report, I've carefully reviewed the advice offered here to make sure it's based on a combination of the latest research and my experience treating patients with OA. (My favorite therapies, supplements, and other approaches are marked in the summary on pages 72–3 with a ★, while other good choices are preceded by a ✔.)

It's important that you try to follow this program as best as you can. You'll be introduced to herbs and supplements that may allow you to reduce the amount of conventional pain medication you take. But an integrative approach doesn't focus on alternatives alone. Here, you'll also learn about lifestyle strategies—the best kinds of exercise for people with OA, foods that might help ease inflammation, techniques to relieve the stress that can make pain worse, and lots of tips for coping with OA from day to day. We've also included plenty of interactive "Try This" activities to ease pain and get control of your OA so you can start taking advantage of the program right away. There's a comprehensive index, selected references, and a resource guide, so you'll be able to stay informed of the latest news on OA long after you've finished reading this book.

I hope that you gain a new sense of empowerment and personal control over OA in these pages, and that this special report becomes a trusted reference in your home health library for years to come.

To your good health,

Andrew Weil, MD

CHAPTER ONE

Understanding Osteoarthritis

Y ou're no stranger to living with stiff, swollen joints—a knee that aches, hip that hurts, or fingers that have difficulty bending. Even simple movements like walking, climbing stairs, and getting out of bed may seem painful. It wasn't always like this. Once, your joints moved smoothly, but then they slowly started to feel creaky and sore. At first, the pain wasn't so bad and eased up when you applied a cold pack or heating pad. It was no big deal. You figured you're getting older and your body just isn't the same as it used to be. But as time passed and the discomfort became a constant part of your life, you realized you needed medical attention.

Now the nagging pain in your joints has a name. Your doctor has diagnosed you with osteoarthritis (OA). *What is this condition?* you wonder. *How will it affect my life?* And, perhaps most important, *How can I ease my pain and keep it from getting worse?*

Fortunately, there are many treatment approaches you can try to relieve the pain. True, there's no magic pill or herb that can make OA disappear altogether. And it's a chronic condition that you'll need to learn how to live with. But by following the diet and exercise guidelines described in this book, experimenting with stress reduction techniques and alternative therapies, and taking conventional pain relievers as needed, you can feel better and take control of your OA.

Actually, the first step to coping with OA is learning what causes the condition and how you may have developed it. Knowing what's going on in your body can help you better understand why your joints feel the way they do. And when you know why you hurt, it's much easier to figure out how to make yourself feel better. In this chapter, you'll learn the basics about what's

"Only I can change my life. No one can do it for me."

CAROL BURNETT

happening in your body when you have OA, how to work with your doctor to put together a treatment plan for it, which pain drugs are most effective, and what other conventional approaches are worth trying.

What Is Osteoarthritis?

The word *arthritis* literally means inflammation of a joint, the place where two bones meet and move. It helps to think of your joints as hinges—and some busy ones at that. They allow you to bend your fingers, elbows, knees, hips, and even open and close your mouth. Because your joints get so much use, they are vulnerable to injury. Unfortunately, Americans are all too familiar

OA vs. RA: What's the Difference?

	Osteoarthritis	Rheumatoid arthritis
Who has it?	Some 20 million American adults, mostly over age 40	Some 2 million American adults, beginning between ages 25 and 50
What's the process?	The breakdown of cartilage and bones, often over decades	Joint inflammation, often developing suddenly within weeks or months
Is it preventable?	Possibly: Maintaining a healthy weight, getting enough exercise, and avoiding joint injury can head off OA.	Maybe, but researchers don't yet know enough about the autoimmune process to offer preventive recommendations.
Autoimmune disorder?	No	Yes
Involves inflammation?	Sometimes	Always
Affects the same joints on both sides of the body?	Sometimes	Often
Causes painful, achy, and stiff joints?	Yes	Yes
Affects other parts of the body?	No	Yes: This systemic disease can also cause fatigue, fever, and, in some cases, can affect the heart, lungs, and membranes surrounding these organs.
Treated with anti-inflammatory drugs?	Yes	Yes
Treated with steroid drugs?	Not usually	Often

with joint inflammation, since about one-third of us suffer from one of some 100 different types of arthritis and related problems, including autoimmune diseases like rheumatoid arthritis and lupus. Some arthritic conditions cause stiffness and pain in just a few areas (like gout, which mainly affects the big toe), while others, such as fibromyalgia, can make your whole body feel achy.

Of all the kinds of arthritis, OA is by far the most common. Even though inflammation is often present in the joints of people with OA, it's not *just* an inflammatory condition. Instead, OA develops when your body progressively loses its cartilage, the slippery material cushioning the ends of bones in a joint. Like a sponge, healthy cartilage fills with and squeezes out a lubricating liquid called synovial fluid whenever your muscles and joints move. Think of cartilage as a sort of shock absorber, much like your car's brake pads: Cartilage allows your bones to glide smoothly over one another without any jarring. But when you have OA, the cartilage becomes dry and starts to wear away. Just as your car's brakes squeal when the brake pads have worn down, cartilage that's dry and disintegrating causes bone to scrape against bone every time you move. Over time, this constant scraping can make the ends of bones become rough like sandpaper and may trigger inflammation in the tissues lining your joints. As a result, ligaments and tendons supporting your joints loosen and surrounding muscles grow weak. When you use the joint, it's sore, achy, and doesn't move as easily as it once did.

You'll most likely notice OA in your joints that do the most work—the ones in your knees, hips, spine, neck, and hands—since the cartilage in these joints undergoes the most wear (see box on page 12). It's also possible to develop it in your shoulders, elbows, wrists, and jaw, especially if you've had a previous injury to those areas, which can cause cartilage to wear away prematurely. You might become more aware of this condition when you have difficulty doing everyday tasks like grasping a pen, bending to lift your grandchild, or rotating your hips as you practice your golf swing. But wherever you feel it, the pain and stiffness of OA can become a constant, unwelcome companion.

How Did You Get Osteoarthritis?

You might think that OA is a fairly recent phenomenon, yet there's evidence that it has been around for quite some time. Believe it or not, scientists have even identified signs of the disease in a 5,000-year-old mummified man! With more people living longer, this undoubtedly will set the stage for more people coping with OA. It's an increasingly common health problem, and if there's

Q&A

Could I have prevented OA?

It's hard to say, since factors you can't control like heredity and gender can influence your risk. But the good news is that you may be able to prevent the *progression* of the disease by maintaining a healthy weight, getting regular exercise, and learning how to use your body in ways that put less stress on your joints—especially when exercising or doing physical work—to protect them from further injury.

Q&A

I have OA. Does this mean my kids could get it, too?

Possibly. Although OA was once thought to be the result of "wear and tear" to the joints, scientists now know that heredity is also involved. In fact, some research shows that people in families with early-onset OA carry a type of genetic mutation that causes the premature breakdown of joint cartilage. And in one large study, scientists followed both parents and their children over several decades to determine their risk for OA. They found that half of the parents and one-third of their adult children had at least one hand joint affected with OA by their 50s and 60s. Interestingly, research also suggests that multiple genes are at work, with different genes responsible for OA in the hands, knees, and hips. All this doesn't necessarily mean your son or daughter will develop OA, but it's a good enough reason for your family members to start some preventive practices now.

comfort in numbers, you're one of more than 20 million Americans currently affected by OA.

OA is on the upswing: By the year 2020, the number of Americans with OA is expected to *double*. That's because record numbers of aging baby boomers will have entered the arthritis-prone years of their 50s and 60s. Even though the pain or other symptoms of OA aren't usually felt until midlife or later, the arthritic process of cartilage wear and bone damage can begin in your joints as early as your 20s, especially if you participate in sports that can stress your joints, like football, soccer, tennis, basketball, and high-impact aerobics. But your age isn't the only factor. Another major reason why OA is on the rise is the increasing number of overweight Americans. Carrying around excess pounds year in and year out certainly takes a toll on your body, especially the joints in your knees and hips.

For most of the last century, researchers believed OA was just a disease of aging that was mainly a result of normal "wear and tear" over the years. But times have changed. While it's true that the condition does involve the wear and tear of cartilage and bones, the process that results in symptoms is no longer thought to be that simple. Within the past several years, scientists have put forth another theory about the causes of OA. This new thinking holds that OA is a complex disorder that may stem from a combination of whole-body and joint-related changes, some of which are still unidentified. That's because not everyone who has OA has suffered a joint injury, is elderly, or is overweight. Changed minds have led to changed descriptions of OA, too. Some researchers have even started referring to OA as "total joint failure"—not exactly the most optimistic description, but one that experts say helps convey the seriousness of the condition by likening it to heart or kidney failure.

Now researchers know that even though age is your biggest risk factor for OA, the condition isn't inevitable. In fact, about 70 percent of people over age 65 show evidence of OA on x-rays, but not all of them have its symptoms. So why do you have them? Chances are, in addition to your age, you also have one of the many other risk factors that scientists believe may play a role in the development of OA. Although the exact causes aren't known, researchers suspect that such triggering factors include repetitive strain of or injuries to your joints (and, therefore, occupations involving lifting, bending, and kneeling), genetics, and gender (more women than men have OA, possibly on account of hormonal differences). Are you a couch potato? If so, your bones and joints can weaken when you don't use them enough. And if you're active, you may have old injuries to the cartilage or ligaments or participate in activities that

Try This: Symptom Diary

Many physicians and pain clinics ask their patients to keep symptom diaries and then share what they've written down with them. Tracking your OA pain and other related complaints along with information about lifestyle factors can help your physician identify what triggers your symptoms and how best to treat them. In a notebook, jot down not only the type of pain you're feeling (grating, aching, soreness, etc.) but also other symptoms you're having that day, like joint stiffness, swelling, fatigue, and limitations in your ability to move and perform certain tasks. Rate your level of symptoms for each part of the day, with 0 being none and 10 being the worst possible. Then write down what you did to try to alleviate symptoms during each period and whether or not it helped. Don't forget to include information on any alternative approaches and self-care you've tried to relieve pain, the dosage of medications and supplements you take, and how much you've exercised. (You can use the sample diary at right for inspiration to get you started.)

Try to make an entry like this at least a few days a week. Looking back at the end of a week or month, you'll perhaps notice some patterns. Maybe the pain gets worse whenever you're upset or better after you've exercised. You might be surprised at how much you didn't know about your pain until you started keeping track of it.

SAMPLE SYMPTOM DIARY ENTRY

Date:	April 7, 2003

MORNING

Type of symptoms:	Stiffness, aching
Severity:	Stiffness, 7; aching, 6
Where?	Right knee
Treatment:	Self massage for 5 minutes; 400 mg ibuprofen; glucosamine supplement; Zostrix cream
How much did it help?	Both symptoms better
Other notes:	Weather is cold and rainy

AFTERNOON

Type of symptoms:	Severe aching
Severity:	9
Where?	Right knee
Treatment:	400 mg ibuprofen; Zostrix cream; deep breathing for 5 minutes
How much did it help?	Aching better but not gone; about level 3
Other notes:	Lots of stress at work

EVENING

Type of symptoms:	Slight stiffness and aching; feel tired
Severity:	Stiffness, 3; aching, 3; fatigue, 5
Where?	Right knee
Treatment:	Went for 20-minute walk; took hot bath afterward
How much did it help?	Stiffness gone; aching about a level 1; fatigue, level 3
Other notes:	Knee always feels better after a walk, and the exercise perks me up

are jarring to your joints, like those sports mentioned on page 10, which can wear down cartilage prematurely.

How did your doctor determine that you have OA? Since there's no single test to detect the disease in its earliest stages, your physician may not have known you had it until you started experiencing symptoms. By now, you're probably all too familiar with the many common symptoms caused by OA, like joint pain or swelling, stiffness, aching, and limited range of motion (decreased mobility). Your doctor may have also given you a physical examination, taken x-rays to determine the amount of joint damage, and ordered blood tests to rule out other health problems. Because science doesn't yet have a foolproof way to tell how bad your pain is, you can help your doctor assess the extent to which your OA has worsened or improved by keeping a diary of your symptoms (see page 11).

Maximizing Your Health Care: An Integrative Approach

Now that you have an understanding of what's happening in your body, you'll be better able to cope with OA on a daily basis. It's important for you to take an active role in your OA treatment and assume responsibility for managing the

Where OA Strikes Most Often

OA can affect any joint, from your jaw to your foot. But the four places where you're most likely to notice the condition are in your hands, hips, knees, and spine. Here's how those areas can be affected:

Hands. Your fingers may become enlarged and bent, and possibly look red. They may feel achy, numb, tender, and stiff. Small, bony knobs can appear on your finger and thumb joints. Eventually, you may lose some ability to grip objects. Hand arthritis occurs most often in older women after menopause, possibly because of hormonal changes.

Hips. OA can strike the joints in one or both hips, resulting in stiffness and pain that may radiate to your groin, buttocks, legs, and knees. When your hips are less flexible, it's harder to bend from the waist and you might even walk with a limp.

Knees. These joints bear much of your body weight and withstand a great deal of pressure and strain. Surprisingly, your knees can remain quite stable until OA reaches an advanced stage when they can become enlarged and stiff. It's possible that you'll feel a grating sensation when you move a knee. Walking, climbing, and getting in and out of chairs and bathtubs may also be difficult.

Spine. The spinal joints or the cartilage in the disks between the bones of your spine is affected. OA of the spine can cause pain and stiffness in the neck, shoulder, or lower back, sometimes with muscle spasms, numbness, or pain that radiates down the arms or legs.

pain. By doing so, you'll have a sense of personal control over your condition, which can improve your ability to function normally and help reduce your level of discomfort. And your doctor has some responsibilities toward you. The two of you should feel like you're working together as a team to discover the particular treatment program that will make you feel your best. In addition, your physician must make the commitment to take your reports of stiffness, soreness, and other symptoms seriously and to listen in a caring and respectful way. This in itself can be very healing.

Ideally, your physician will be open to integrative approaches to OA, like the judicious use of supplements, mind-body techniques, alternative therapies, and the other measures described in this book. The majority of arthritis patients now say they use one or more of these approaches, so most doctors are aware of—if not necessarily well-versed in—integrative options. As you read this book, share the sections that most interest you with your physician. Tell your doctor which approaches and supplements you plan to try and how you think they might help, whether it's to relieve pain or reduce stress. That way, your physician can chart your progress, catch possible supplement and drug interactions, and even adjust your dose of pain medication if necessary.

Conventional Care for Osteoarthritis

Once you've been diagnosed with OA, your physician—or sometimes a rheumatologist, a doctor who specializes in managing pain and inflammation—will suggest treatment. There isn't yet a cure for OA and the condition won't disappear altogether, so conventional doctors focus on helping to relieve symptoms like pain, decreased mobility, and perhaps inflammation. Among its many benefits, treatment can help ease stiffness in knees, relieve soreness in hips, and make it easier to grasp a pen or move your neck without pain. To accomplish these goals, your doctor will probably talk to you about taking over-the-counter (OTC) or prescription drugs, undergoing physical therapy, getting enough exercise (see page 25), or a combination of these approaches. These treatments are also part of the *Self Healing* program for OA. Here's what you can expect from each of these conventional treatments.

MEDICATION

In general, there are three main kinds of pain-relieving medications that your doctor might suggest you take. Here's the lowdown on these drugs, in the order in which they're often recommended to people with OA.

Q&A

I tend to crack my knuckles. Did this cause my OA?

Cracking your knuckles (or neck or other joints) doesn't appear to *cause* the condition, but it may have put you at higher risk for OA of the hands. When you pull on your knuckles, the bones in your fingers are pulled apart and nitrogen gas in the joint fluid is displaced, creating little bubbles that cause a popping or cracking sound when they burst. In larger joints, like those in your neck or back, ligaments moving over bone can produce this noise. Actually, the only study done on knuckle-cracking and OA found no association between the two, but non-crackers had a stronger hand grip than those with the habit. Cracking a joint repeatedly *can* do harm: It can lead to long-term damage by overstretching ligaments or creating friction in the joints, both of which may predispose you to OA. In any case, it's probably a good idea to lay off this bad habit and find healthier ways to reduce tension.

Acetaminophen. For relatively mild pain, your doctor may start your OA treatment program by suggesting that you take the OTC drug acetaminophen (Tylenol). Doctors like acetaminophen because it irritates the stomach less than NSAIDs (see below). Sounds good, but, unfortunately, acetaminophen doesn't help with joint inflammation, so if that's one of your symptoms, you might not find this painkiller helpful. In fact, one study found that acetaminophen is no more effective than a placebo in relieving the pain of knee OA (*Archives of Internal Medicine*, January 27, 2003).

NSAIDs. If acetaminophen doesn't help, your doctor may suggest that you take OTC nonsteroidal anti-inflammatory drugs (NSAIDs) such as ibuprofen, aspirin, and naproxen instead. NSAIDs are also available in higher doses by prescription. You'll probably find that NSAIDs help ease your symptoms somewhat; they're quite effective at short-term relief of mild to moderate pain and inflammation. But NSAIDs can also irritate your stomach and intestines and even cause severe gastrointestinal (GI) effects, like ulcers and bleeding. Be sure to tell your doctor if you've had stomach pain after taking an NSAID.

> DR. WEIL SAYS: "While I think over-the-counter NSAIDs are fine to use as needed for short-term relief of mild to moderate pain, I think it's more important to implement lifestyle strategies that can have a greater long-term impact on OA."

COX-2 inhibitors. If NSAIDs bother your stomach, your doctor might switch you to a COX-2 inhibitor. You've probably heard about these newer prescription drugs, including Celebrex, since they've been aggressively advertised for relieving OA pain without causing GI problems. Like traditional NSAIDs, COX-2 inhibitors reduce your body's production of prostaglandins, hormonelike substances made by two enzymes called COX-1 and COX-2. Prostaglandins made by COX-1 protect your stomach lining, while those made by COX-2 cause pain and inflammation. Traditional NSAIDs inhibit both the COX-1 and COX-2 enzymes, relieving pain but also promoting GI problems. Celebrex inhibits only the COX-2 enzymes. In other words, it helps ease pain but presumably spares your stomach.

Are these so-called super-aspirins all they're cracked up to be? Not exactly. Celebrex is really only as effective as traditional NSAIDs at relieving pain and inflammation. While its benefit supposedly lies in its ability to protect your GI lining, there's not a lot of good scientific evidence to back this up. In fact, one major study of Celebrex—which claimed to find a lower risk of ulcers in people taking the drug—has been criticized for omitting data that showed it had no such benefit. And Celebrex isn't free of other side effects: It can trigger coughing, fever, and a sore throat, and may worsen asthma as well as kidney or liver disease. Another big drawback is its price: Celebrex is expensive—it can cost up to $140 for a 30-day supply, compared to about $10 for over-the-counter aspirin or ibuprofen. In short, it's best to use COX-2 inhibitors only if you're at high risk for stomach problems; for example, if you're over age 75 and have a history of GI bleeding.

DR. WEIL SAYS: "If you have osteoarthritis, I'd try natural COX-2 inhibitors like ginger and turmeric before resorting to Celebrex, or even traditional NSAIDs. These herbs show promise in relieving pain and inflammation in much the same way as prescription COX-2 inhibitors, but without their side effects." (See page 53 for more.)

Q&A

Will my OA ever go away?

OA is a degenerative disease that may worsen with time, and currently there's no cure for it. On the bright side, though, there are plenty of measures you can take to slow its progression and minimize symptoms. In severe cases, surgical replacement of joints in the hip, knee, or other affected areas can eliminate OA at those sites.

PHYSICAL THERAPY

If you've ever broken a bone or wrenched your back, you've probably had physical therapy (PT) to help you heal faster and learn how to safely start moving again. PT can also be extremely helpful for OA, especially in the knee, hip, or foot, by relieving pain, strengthening your muscles, improving your ability to move your joints with ease, and preventing disability. When you have OA, you'll probably want to use a painful joint less, but staying sedentary will only further weaken it. Under the supervision of a physical therapist, you can discover ways to keep your joints in motion, despite any current limitations. In fact, regular use of PT is a natural, drug-free treatment that can ease your aching and may even reduce your need for surgery.

Your doctor can refer you to a physical therapist, who will use a variety of different approaches to keep your joints active and pain-free. (Most health insurance plans cover PT for a limited number of sessions or a set amount of time; check your policy.) First, you'll likely learn some stretching, strengthening, and aerobic exercises to help you build strong and flexible muscles, which in turn support and protect your joints. These methods can also build your stamina, so you'll have less fatigue and more energy as you go about your day. You might also be taught techniques to improve your coordination and balance, two key elements in preventing falls and minimizing injuries. Your therapist will show you how to continue doing the exercises on your own at home, and you may do them instead of or in addition to your regular fitness routine.

Occasionally, PT includes movement re-education techniques as well. Some physical therapists are also practitioners of the Alexander Technique or Feldenkrais Method, therapies that focus on teaching you how to change incorrect patterns of movement and improve your posture. Typically, though, PT aims to restore movement you once had in your joints, rather than teach you new ways of moving altogether. After you complete a month or two of PT, you might want to consider consulting a practitioner of the Alexander Technique or Feldenkrais Method (see pages 46 and 48) to further improve your ability to move without pain.

Exercise is rehabilitative, but PT includes other treatment modalities that can also help. After you complete some exercises, your therapist may apply a hot or cold pack, massage your joints, or have you soak in a heated pool or whirlpool, all of which can relieve soreness and minor pain. Ultrasound—high-frequency sound waves to bring heat to deeper muscles—might also be used. Sometimes, your joints may feel worse than usual. On those days, your physical therapist might use TENS therapy, which relies on the electrical stimulation of nerve endings in joints to temporarily relieve pain. PT may sometimes include a prescription for temporary stabilizing braces or splints that you wear on your arthritic joints to keep you from moving them beyond a comfortable range of motion.

All in all, PT can help ease OA symptoms and may lessen your reliance on medication. If you do the exercises at home, outside of your appointments, they can make a world of difference in the way you move and feel.

CHAPTER TWO

Eating Well with Osteoarthritis

When you're faced with a future of achy joints and pain medications, you might wonder if you could relieve your symptoms by eating or avoiding certain foods and beverages. For some medical conditions, there's an obvious connection between food and health, such as when a chili dog gives you heartburn or when ice cream triggers a headache. The link between diet and osteoarthritis is less clear. There just isn't a lot of good scientific evidence that food can improve or worsen OA symptoms, but it's a hot topic of debate among scientists.

Actually, the kind of food you consume may be less important to OA than the *amount* of it you eat. There is a connection between maintaining a healthy weight and a reduced risk of the disease. One of the most important dietary strategies you can follow to ease OA is to avoid being overweight, since excess pounds put additional strain on your joints. Believe it or not, every extra pound you gain can feel like an extra three pounds of pressure to your knees and hips. This added stress on the joints means that people who are overweight are at much greater risk of developing OA, and of having the disease progress, than those who are slim. In fact, being severely overweight is linked to half of all cases of osteoarthritis of the knee and about a quarter of cases in the hip. You might assume overweight people could have problems with too much stress on weight-bearing joints such as the knees and hips, but they're also more likely to have OA in other joints—in the hands, neck, or elbows, for example—suggesting some systemic, whole-body effect of obesity as well.

People who are extremely heavy aren't the only ones who need to watch their weight. Even those who could stand to lose 20 pounds are straining their joints, meaning that their OA is likely to get worse sooner than it would have

> "Never eat more than you can lift."
>
> MISS PIGGY

if they weighed less. What's the good news? If you're overweight, even a small weight loss can make a big difference in how you feel: In one large study, people who lost just 10 pounds or more in the decade before the study began cut their risk of osteoarthritis of the knee in half. Other research suggests that even if you already have OA, achieving a healthy weight can help relieve pain and other symptoms.

> **DR. WEIL SAYS:** "At various points in my life, I too have struggled with my weight. Based on my experience and that of my patients, my own advice for losing weight has long been to eat less and exercise more. That is, you have to burn more calories through exercise than you take in through eating. The good news is that you don't have to starve yourself or become a fitness fanatic in order to shed pounds."

Staying Slim to Ease OA Symptoms

Losing pounds *sensibly* is the key to achieving and maintaining a healthy weight. More to the point, you shouldn't try to drop a lot of weight quickly through fad diets or supplements, since you're likely to gain back any weight you lose. Instead, set realistic goals. You might not drop four clothing sizes, but losing and keeping off just 10 pounds—over the course of several months—could take a big load off your joints. And there's no need to weigh yourself constantly: Once a week is fine. Here are three key strategies for losing weight.

Eat a healthy diet. To lose weight, you must reduce the *amount* of food you eat, both by decreasing portion sizes and cutting down on snacking. But it still makes sense to get about 50 to 60 percent of your calories as carbohydrate, 30 percent as fat, and 10 to 20 percent as protein. You don't have to follow a very-low-fat diet, but make sure the fats you consume are healthy ones (see page 22). Here's more advice on what to eat and what to avoid:

• *Eat plenty of fruits, vegetables, whole grains, and beans.* These high-quality, fiber-rich foods tend to be filling but low in calories. They're also excellent sources of complex carbohydrates, which are best for weight control.

• *Avoid refined carbs.* Refined carbohydrates—foods made with sugar and white flour—are now believed to be one of the major dietary contributors to obesity. These foods rate high on the glycemic index (GI), which measures how easily your body turns a particular food into glucose (blood sugar). High-GI foods can provoke insulin secretion and, in many people, increase the tendency to store excess calories as body fat. And so-called diet foods might actually be sabotaging your weight loss. Some, like rice cakes, crispbread, and low-fat cookies, cakes, and frozen desserts, are often high in refined carbohydrates, even though they're low in calories. For a glycemic-index listing of common foods, see *www.glycemicindex.com* or *The Glucose Revolution* by Jennie Brand-Miller et al. (Marlowe & Co., 1999).

　• *Drink lots of water.* Water has no calories, is filling, and is more healthful than diet soda, sugary drinks, or alcoholic beverages. Another plus: Drinking six to eight glasses of good-quality water each day can also help lubricate and nourish stiff joints.

　• *Avoid artificial sweeteners and fake fats.* There's no evidence that artificial sweeteners or products made with them help anyone lose weight, and the same goes for snack foods made with the fat substitute olestra. If you want to snack, reach for fresh fruit, vegetable sticks, a handful of nuts, even a piece of dark chocolate if you crave a sweet.

Pay Attention to Portion Sizes

Whether you're trying to lose weight to alleviate an achy knee—or just for general good health—you'll need to pay attention to the portion sizes of your food, which take into account both *what* you eat and drink and *how much*. Actually, if you're like most people, you've been overestimating the amount of food that makes up a true portion. Once you've got a good idea of the amount you're eating and drinking, however, you'll find it easier to make a conscious effort to reduce your portion sizes.

Know a portion from a serving. A portion is the actual amount of food that's right for you—for your age, gender, activity level, and health needs. On the other hand, a serving is simply a unit of measure. For example, a "serving" recommended by the Food Guide Pyramid may seem skimpy when you realize that one-half cup of cooked pasta equals one bread serving, making it easy to get six bread servings with a typical restaurant plate of pasta. In addition, know that a serving on a food label is for comparison shopping and may not be the same as a Pyramid serving.

Train your eyes. First, figure out which foods or beverages are supplying you with the most calories. Common culprits are starchy, fatty, and sugary foods. Next, weigh and measure some common serving sizes. Then place a reasonable portion on your plate or in your bowl. You'll also want to find out how much liquid your glassware and mugs can hold, and identify a four- and eight-ounce serving. Try to form a mental snapshot of these quantities.

Use visual cues. A quick way to gauge an appropriate portion of meat or fish is to compare it to the size of your palm or a deck of cards. For starchy side dishes or a medium fruit, your portion should be about the size of a tennis ball, while one ounce of cheese is comparable to four dice.

Revamp your plate. Plant-based foods can easily displace other, higher-calorie foods on your plate. Ideally, vegetables should take up at least half of your dinner plate, while grains and a protein source (such as fish, soy foods, beans, or poultry) equally make up the remaining half. Another way to eat smaller portions and not feel deprived is to use a salad plate rather than a dinner plate.

Fewer Pounds in a Pill?

You've been working hard to lose weight by eating a healthy diet and exercising regularly, but the pounds don't seem to be coming off fast enough. Or maybe you lost weight when you first started dieting but have reached a plateau and feel stuck. Without a doubt, weight loss is hard work, and lots of people yearn for a "quick fix." To fill the bill, there's an ever-expanding market for miracle-diet books, plans, and pills that promise easy weight loss.

Unfortunately, there are no magic bullets. Truth is, people who lose weight on fad diets typically regain whatever pounds they dropped once they go off their eating plans. Likewise, diet products containing stimulant drugs (such as ephedrine and synephrine) or stimulant herbs (ephedra, guaraná, and kola nut) may promote short-term weight loss by affecting metabolism, but your weight will rapidly rebound when you stop taking them. All such stimulants are addictive and have potentially harmful side effects. The heart-racing effects of ephedra in particular have been linked to heart attacks, strokes, and deaths, prompting calls for legislation to ban it. As for the prescription weight-loss drugs on the market, they may work only very modestly and can be toxic.

DR. WEIL SAYS: "You're more likely to succeed at managing your weight if you do it for yourself, to feel healthier and not to meet others' expectations. Success is also more likely if you concentrate on gradually adopting healthier habits and maintaining them for the long term. Congratulate yourself for each walk you take, each fruit or vegetable you eat, or each time you manage your 'emotional' hunger in ways other than food."

Manage your hunger. Approaching weight loss with a mindset of deprivation sets you up to fail. Instead, find a way to eat less while managing your physical and emotional hunger. As you reach for food, ask yourself whether you're truly hungry or just eating out of habit, boredom, or stress. Below you'll find out ways to manage your hunger and control your portions:

• *Initially, count calories.* For a week or two, estimate your average daily caloric intake by consulting food labels or calorie-counter books. This will give you a clearer picture of how much you're truly eating and can help you learn how much your body really needs to be healthy and satisfied. When trying to lose weight, women should go no lower than 1,200 calories per day, men no lower than 1,500 calories, to ensure adequate nutrition.

• *Keep a food diary.* Writing down what you eat can make you more mindful of your eating habits and keep you honest. For a few weeks or more, try recording every food and beverage you consume, the portion size, and when you consumed it. Many people also find that keeping a diary of their physical activity helps them keep moving and stay motivated. If you like, combine this information with the details from your symptom diary (see page 11) to get a clearer picture of how lifestyle changes affect your OA.

• *Develop a sense of appropriate portions.* Reading labels can help, but at first you may want to measure out foods and even weigh them until you become a better judge of portion size. (See the box on page 19 for more.)

• *Eat mindfully.* If you're not paying attention to what you're putting in your mouth, it's easy to overeat. Don't watch TV or read the newspaper while you eat. Chew your food thoroughly, and practice putting your fork or spoon down between bites. Eating mindfully can help you enjoy your food more and feel satisfied sooner.

• *Control emotional eating.* The stress of living with chronic pain may make you reach for food when you're feeling down. Instead, try doing the Relaxing Breath exercise (see page 38). By the time you finish this exercise, your craving may well have passed.

Get regular exercise. Burning calories through physical activity is an essential part of any successful weight-loss (and weight-maintenance) program, and can definitely help reduce the symptoms of OA. For more on exercise, see page 25.

Eating an "Anti-Arthritis" Diet

From a dietary standpoint, your best bet to lessen the pain of arthritic joints is to achieve and maintain a healthy weight. But it also doesn't hurt to try to eat a sensible diet like the one described here—that's rich in fresh fruits and vegetables, whole grains, legumes, healthy monounsaturated and omega-3 fats, and plant sources of protein like tofu, soymilk, and other soy foods. Substituting such foods for less healthy options like meat, full-fat milk, butter, and other dairy products, as well as processed snack foods, is great for your waistline, good for your heart, and may even benefit your OA.

There is one area of research on diet and OA that shows promise: It seems that people who eat foods rich in certain vitamins have milder OA symptoms than those who don't. For example, vitamins C and E and beta-carotene are antioxidants that fight free radicals, compounds that can damage your cartilage. Some research has found that people with knee OA who consume about 150 mg of vitamin C each day have less pain and slower progression of OA than those who don't. Other studies suggest that people who get at least 9,000 IU of beta-carotene and 400 IU of vitamin E daily are at a reduced risk for their OA progressing and may experience less pain and improved ease of movement than people who consume lower amounts. And while it's not an antioxidant, vitamin D is crucial for good bone strength and structure, as well as healthy cartilage. Consuming about 400 IU of vitamin D a day has been shown to decrease the risk of OA's worsening.

Although most of these studies looked at the amount of these nutrients that people with OA took in from *food*, it's not a bad idea to supplement with vitamins and minerals as insurance. In addition to following the healthy diet described, try taking 200 mg of vitamin C, 400 to 800 IU of natural vitamin E (people over age 65 need 800 IU) or 80 mg of vitamin E with tocopherols and tocotrienols , 25,000 IU of mixed carotenes (which include beta-carotene), and 400 IU of vitamin D daily. You can take these supplements separately, or you may find them all in a high-quality multivitamin, multimineral supplement.

Finally, in addition to getting enough antioxidants, you might find it helpful to include more foods in your diet that reduce inflammation, such as

Omega-3s: Not Just a Fish Tale

It's true that oily, cold-water fish like salmon and sardines are great sources of omega-3 fatty acids, which can reduce OA-related inflammation. But they're not the only foods with these healthy fats. Here are some other tasty ways to include more omega-3s in your diet.

Flax seeds. Buy whole flax seeds at a health food store, store them in the refrigerator, and grind a half-cup or so at a time, using an electric coffee grinder dedicated to this purpose. Ground flax has a nutty flavor and tastes delicious sprinkled over cereals, salads, baked potatoes, and other vegetables. Plus, you can bake the flax meal into muffins or bread, which won't affect the omega-3 content (but heating flax makes it more susceptible to spoilage). Refrigerate flax meal in an airtight container—it will keep for up to 30 days.

Walnuts. An excellent source of omega-3s, walnuts are great to snack on raw, or try adding them to salads. Walnut oil makes great salad dressings.

Fortified eggs. Several companies sell eggs that contain omega-3s as a result of special mash fed to the hens. Unfortunately, you'd have to eat several eggs each day to get optimal levels of omega-3s. Instead, limit yourself to an average of one fortified egg a day while also getting omega-3s from oily fish or flax.

salmon and other oily, cold-water fish, flaxseed, walnuts, produce, and olive oil, and to avoid or eliminate those that promote inflammation (many processed foods, margarine, and vegetable oils). Eating such a diet may theoretically help ease achy joints, and it may reduce your risk of cancer and benefit your overall health as well. In general, you should try to:

Get More...

Omega-3 fatty acids. These special fats are called "essential fatty acids" because they can't be made by your body and must come from the food you eat. Your body uses the omega-3s you consume to make hormones that keep inflammation from getting out of control. Clearly, that can be a big help for anyone with OA. So if you want to help ease inflamed joints, you'll need to get optimal levels of omega-3s: That means aiming for three or more 3-ounce servings of oily fish (such as salmon or sardines) a week, plus another source of omega-3s (such as walnuts or flax seeds) on other days. If you're a vegetarian, eat 2 tablespoons of ground flax seeds a day, and try to eat other omega-3 sources (like walnuts or fortified eggs) regularly. Sure, these recommendations may seem high, but you can work your way up to them gradually.

DR. WEIL SAYS: "Dietary fat is a buzzword today. We've been told for years that fat is evil and that it's desirable to eat as little of it as possible. I disagree with all those ideas. Fat is an essential nutrient, and I think that a healthy diet can include it, as long as you're eating the right kinds of fat."

Fruits and vegetables. Who can resist biting into a peach running with juice, or nibbling on perfect ears of sweet corn? Fresh produce is delicious, and, even better, it may make a difference in how your joints feel. That's because fruits and vegetables contain antioxidants, vitamins and minerals that may help neutralize the free radicals believed to cause the inflammation and joint damage associated with OA. Try to eat 5 to 9 daily servings of antioxidant-rich produce, including squash, melons, carrots, berries, and citrus fruits.

Olive oil. This monounsaturated fat may help ease joint inflammation, since it contains an anti-inflammatory substance called squalene and is rich in vitamin E, which also shows promise for treating arthritis. Make extra-virgin olive oil your main cooking oil, whether you're stir-frying or baking.

Ginger and turmeric. These tasty spices serve double duty: They're flavorful ingredients and also effective natural anti-inflammatory agents that may help ease OA pain. Try adding moderate amounts of ginger and turmeric to your meals: Ginger's sweet and pungent flavor is delicious in Asian dishes, fruit compotes, and, of course, gingerbread, while turmeric's strong, bitter flavor spices up curries, chutneys, rice, and other Indian dishes.

Water. The squishy cartilage that cushions your joints is 70 percent water, which moisturizes them and helps carry oxygen and other nutrients to all body parts. Ideally, you'll want to drink at least eight 8-ounce glasses of water a day. It sounds like a lot, but it's not hard to drink this much once you start substituting water for coffee, alcohol, soft drinks, and other less-healthy beverages. (So far, there's no good evidence that caffeine or alcohol can worsen OA, but they certainly won't help and alcohol is a source of empty calories.)

And Eat Fewer Foods Containing...

Partially hydrogenated oils. Manufacturers love to use them to extend the shelf-life of doughnuts, snack cakes, and French fries, but partially hydrogenated oils and other sources of trans fatty acids can damage the heart as well as promote inflammation, possibly worsening your arthritis pain. Do your best to avoid foods with these fats, which you'll also find in some margarines, potato chips, cookies, crackers, and many other processed foods. Read labels!

Polyunsaturated vegetable oils. They've got the word "vegetable" in their name, so these oils must be healthy, right? Wrong. Polyunsaturated vegetable oils, which include safflower, sunflower, and corn oils, contain omega-6 fatty acids. While some scientists believe we need omega-6s and omega-3s at a ratio of about 2:1 or ideally 1:1 to keep important body functions in balance, the ratio in the typical American diet is closer to 10:1 or more. This imbalance may increase inflammation, which is troublesome for people with OA. Cut back on omega-6s while increasing your intake of omega-3s.

What about Food Sensitivities?

Wouldn't it be great if simply avoiding a particular food could ease arthritic joints? Unfortunately, we don't yet know whether specific foods can worsen any kind of arthritis other than gout, a condition that can cause joint pain, typically in the big toe. In people with gout, foods that are high in compounds called purines (like red meat, shellfish, and lentils) seem to exacerbate the disease, while avoiding them can help ward off pain. Also, some people with

OA in the Kitchen

As long as you're relatively active, OA shouldn't have a big effect on your *appetite* for food. However, cooking can become difficult for some people, especially when the disease affects the hands. If gripping spoons, using knives, opening jars, or performing similar movements is a problem, consider investing in some arthritis-friendly kitchen gadgets and tools (see page 67 for more). You can also make meal preparation easier by sharing responsibilities with a family member or making large batches of food to freeze for later, which can cut down on your time spent in the kitchen.

rheumatoid arthritis find that eliminating certain foods, such as dairy products, or abstaining from food altogether for short periods of time (fasting), helps them, but these practices seem to have no effect on OA.

On the other hand, some people with either rheumatoid arthritis or osteoarthritis say that eating foods in the nightshade family seems to influence these conditions. In fact, avoiding nightshade vegetables—tomatoes, potatoes, peppers, and eggplant—was once a popular dietary recommendation for OA. There is little scientific basis for this dietary approach, since very few people appear to have true sensitivities to—and therefore worsened OA symptoms from—these foods. What's more, some nightshades can be difficult to avoid, such as paprika, a spice made from sweet peppers that's common in prepared foods. Still, if you find that eating such foods increases your pain, you might try phasing them out of your diet one at a time and see whether it helps.

CHAPTER THREE

Keep Moving with Osteoarthritis

I f your joints are hurting, the last thing you may feel like doing is exercising. But getting regular physical activity is one of nature's best "medicines" for OA, and it's now an important part of any treatment program for healthier joints. This wasn't always the case. As recently as 20 years ago, doctors advised people with OA to *rest* their bodies completely—up to six months of bed rest was recommended—as a way to prevent further joint damage. Today, physicians recognize that being active encourages the production and flow of lubricating joint fluid, builds muscle strength, and eases painful joints, while being sedentary makes your joints feel even stiffer and shrinks your muscles.

To emphasize the importance of regular physical activity to their patients with OA, some physicians have started writing out exercise recommendations on a prescription pad, which they hope will be followed with the same faithfulness as taking a needed medication. In many ways, the benefits of a regular fitness program for OA are comparable to—and probably less expensive than— those of a drug. But *not* being active can be detrimental to your health: If you don't keep moving despite having OA, the joint and its surrounding muscles and tendons weaken. This makes the joint itself less stable, and the muscles can subsequently tighten and shorten, which limits your mobility. As discussed in the previous chapter, regular exercise can ease the burden on already damaged joints, in part by helping you achieve or maintain a healthy weight. In addition, being active not only tones up your body, it can even brighten your mood. Exercise offers so many benefits to OA that it makes sense to "just do it."

According to the American Council on Exercise's suggested regimen for

> "Nothing is more revealing than movement."
>
> MARTHA GRAHAM

people with arthritis, you should aim for three kinds of activity:

• *Aerobic exercise* three to five times a week for general conditioning, gradually working up to at least 20 minutes per session.

• *Strength training* two or three times a week to build the muscles that give a joint stability and protect it from unnecessary stress.

• *Stretching and range-of-motion exercises* done daily to ease stiffness and gently improve mobility.

Exercising in comfortably warm water is a great way for people with OA to include these three elements of fitness in one workout. And compared to land-based activities, the buoyancy of water can make once-painful moves much easier (see page 32 for more). You might not consider yourself much of an athlete, but just start with whatever activity you can do easily that might be fun, and gradually spend more time doing it. The more you exercise, the more benefits you'll see in the long run.

Safety First: Exercising with OA

Exercise can be safe and effective for people with OA, but it's still important to check first with your doctor if you haven't exercised regularly before or are starting a new fitness program. (One special concern: If you also have high blood pressure, you must get it under control before starting a strength training program, as blood pressure can rise dramatically during this form of exercise.) Of course, you'll also want to make sure that you've got the right gear. Choose shoes that are lightweight and flexible, and buy them late in the day, when your feet are at their largest. Most sporting goods stores also carry socks made of materials that help wick away perspiration and prevent blisters.

Once you begin exercising, take it slow, starting with just a few minutes of aerobic activity or one or two strength training exercises. It's a good idea to build up to your goal over an eight-week period. For the first few weeks, try to exercise 10 minutes a day; then extend it to 15; and eventually 20; and so on. In time, you can gradually work up to the recommended workouts mentioned below. No matter what type of exercise you try or how long you do it, warm up first for a couple of minutes by walking slowly, for example, to get your muscles and joints moving.

You might wish to consult a physical therapist or personal trainer, who can develop a fitness program tailored to your individual needs and goals, teach you the proper techniques, and monitor your progress. And if you're interested in arthritis-specific exercise classes, ask your local Arthritis

Foundation chapter about their PACE (People with Arthritis Can Exercise) program. Participants in the PACE program do gentle aerobic, strength training, and flexibility exercises in order to improve mobility, whether they're able-bodied or using a wheelchair, cane, or other assistive device. Getting regular physical activity might not completely eliminate arthritis-related pain, but it may help it subside and become easier to tolerate, since your body is stronger. Here are more details on what should make up an ideal exercise program for people with OA.

Aerobic Activity (20 to 30 minutes, three to five days per week)

Doing aerobic activity may sound like it requires a leotard and gym membership, but it really means doing anything that gets your heart beating faster and your breath going. Actually, the word *aerobic* means "with oxygen," since it improves your heart's ability to deliver nourishing oxygen to your muscles. By walking briskly, running, dancing, swimming, cycling, or even completing your household chores, you'll strengthen your heart, lungs, and muscles. Plus, you'll burn calories and increase your stamina—the ability to keep moving without tiring out. But you don't need to run a marathon or climb a mountain: Research has shown that previously sedentary and obese adults who learn to integrate moderate-intensity activities into their daily lives—such as brisk walking and raking leaves—experience similar health and fitness benefits as those who engage in more vigorous—and joint-stressing—aerobics programs. Here are some types of aerobic activity to try—or to avoid—if you have OA.

Cycling. You might think that riding a bike would be too painful for arthritic knees, but just the opposite is true. Because cycling takes the weight off your leg joints, it's actually a great aerobic activity to start with if you find walking or other forms of exercise too uncomfortable. Don't worry if you don't own a bike or aren't crazy about riding outdoors: You'll get similar benefits pedaling inside on a stationary bicycle. In fact, indoor exercise bikes come in both upright and recumbent (partially reclined) versions; recumbent bikes, which include backrests, may be more comfortable if you have OA of the spine or other back problems.

Dancing. Professional ballet dancers have a higher risk of OA, but less-intense dance forms shouldn't be a problem. Ballroom dancing, square dancing, line dancing, and even belly dancing are great ways to get a fun aerobic workout set to music, and their gliding motions help keep stiff joints moving.

Elliptical trainers. These machines provide a similar aerobic workout to

In the Swing of Things

You don't have to give up golfing just because you have OA. In fact, golf can easily be adapted for people with physical limitations, including OA. Golf can even *benefit* your joints: Practicing your swing can strengthen your arms, legs, hips, and spine, and takes your joints through their full range of motion. Plus, golf pro shops sell lighter weight clubs, special grips, and other products that can help make the sport easier on your joints.

running, but the gliding, oval-shaped motion done on an elliptical trainer is far less jarring to your joints, especially because your feet never leave the pedals. And the same is true of the fluid movement done on cross-country ski machines. You may find these machines in health clubs; they're also available for home use, although they can be pricey. Cross-country skiing and snowshoeing outdoors in winter weather are other good options.

Rowing. Whether you're on a machine or on the water, rowing is good aerobic exercise. But its back-and-forth motion can be hard on arthritic knee and elbow joints.

Running. Conventional wisdom holds that running and jogging can stress your knee joints, putting you at higher risk for OA. In truth, studies of running and risk of OA are mixed. Right now, it seems that serious athletes who follow a rigorous running regimen may have an increased risk of developing knee and hip OA, but casual joggers who run two or three times a week aren't. If you do jog, be sure to warm up before and stretch after your run to avoid injury, which can raise your risk of OA.

Skiing. The jarring motions, bumpy terrain, and chance of falling make downhill skiing less than ideal for people with OA. A better choice is cross-country skiing, which gives you a great aerobic workout without stressing your joints.

Step machines. You can get a good workout from stair-stepping machines, but you'll need to use them cautiously—if at all—when you have knee OA. That's because step machines can put a lot of stress on your knee joints, since you must bend your knees more than you would when using an elliptical trainer or bicycle.

Swimming. Because water supports most of your body weight, swimming takes the weight off of your joints, making it a great activity for people with OA. Water aerobics, especially those classes designed for people with arthritis, and water walking are also good choices (see page 32 for more).

Tennis. Tennis and other racquet sports provide a great aerobic workout, but the jarring, stop-and-start motions they require can put a lot of stress on your wrist, knee, and ankle joints. People who play racquet sports are also at risk for tennis elbow, a painful inflammation of the tendons. If you wish to continue playing tennis, choose a grass court rather than asphalt one, which is less stressful to your knees.

Walking. Putting one foot in front of the other doesn't require any fancy gear or special skills. Plus, walking can be done anywhere and has the least risk of injury of any form of activity. Even people with OA in the knees can walk regularly, although you may want to avoid steep hills (which stress the knees) and use a walking stick or cane for assistance. The slightly cushioned surface of a treadmill can also make walking easier for people with OA. To get the most aerobic benefit from your walk, you'll need to move at a brisk pace, eventually working up to a 15-minute mile (about 4 miles per hour).

DR. WEIL SAYS: "I walk as much for pleasure as for my health: Here in Arizona, I often take my Rhodesian ridgeback dogs (or rather, they take me) along a hilly, cactus-strewn path through Saguaro National Park next to my ranch, setting out in early morning when it's hot or in the afternoon during the cooler part of the year. When I'm traveling, I'd rather tackle the hills of San Francisco or people-watch on the streets of New York than go to a gym."

Strength Training (20 minutes, two to three times a week)

You might think that heavy lifting is the worst thing you can do for your joints, but training with weights appropriate to your ability can actually ease stiffness, build muscle, and make joints stronger and suppler. Although strength training isn't considered an aerobic activity, it can still benefit your health in many ways. Gaining more muscle means you'll lose more fat, since strong muscles boost your metabolism, helping you burn calories faster. Strength training can also slow and even reverse many other age-related problems, such as fatigue, poor balance, difficulty walking, and dependence on others for assistance with daily chores.

A typical full-body strength training program consists of about 8 to 12 exercises designed to work your body's major muscle groups—arms, shoulders, chest, abdomen, back, buttocks, hips, and legs. You can strengthen these muscles with exercises like biceps curls, leg presses, back extensions, and sit-ups, to name a few. Of course, you should ask your physical therapist, personal trainer, or other fitness professional which exercises are the safest and least desirable for you to try, depending on which of your joints are arthritic. You'll want to strength train two to three days a week, taking a break at least one day in between so that your muscles can rest. As for equipment, options include:

Free weights. No, you don't need to lift the large barbells used by professional bodybuilders to strengthen your muscles. Actually, most people lifting for general fitness purposes usually use hand weights (known as dumbbells) and/or ankle weights. The weight you lift should be heavy enough to challenge you without causing injury—you may feel sore after your first few workouts, but you shouldn't feel pain. Each lift and lowering of a weight is called a repetition, or "rep." It should take you at least 7 seconds to complete each rep: 2 seconds to lift the weight up, 1 second to hold it in an upright position, and 4 seconds to lower it back down. Choose a weight that you can lift at least eight times; the eighth rep should be difficult to do. If you can perform more than 15 reps in a row without difficulty, it's time to start gradually increasing the weight. Planning to work out at home? Invest in pairs of 3-, 5-, and 8-pound dumbbells. In a pinch, you can use a roll of quarters or soup can, then work up to heavier weights. And don't let hand OA stand in your way. If you find gripping free weights difficult, try using Velcro-fastening ankle weights attached to your wrists instead.

Weight machines. After some basic explanation from a fitness instructor or physical therapist, it's easy to learn how to use weight machines. And they limit your range of motion, reducing your risk of joint and muscle injury. Popular brands are Nautilus and Cybex.

Rubber tubing. Lightweight and portable, rubber tubing and giant rubber exercise bands let you perform a range of exercises for both your upper and lower body, and can be found at many sporting goods stores.

Stability balls. Also known as Swiss exercise balls and physioballs, these inflatable plastic orbs can help stretch and strengthen your muscles. Just sitting on a stability ball, with your back straight and legs wide apart while you hold in your stomach and gently and slowly bounce, can strengthen your hamstrings, quadriceps, and abdominal and back muscles. It's best for people with OA to choose an oblong (rather than round) ball, which offers more stability for weak joints. You can find stability balls at some department stores, sporting goods stores, and Internet retailers.

Resistance exercises. You may not even need any special equipment, since exercises like squats, lunges, pushups, and sit-ups use your own body weight to increase strength. However, you'll want to consult your doctor or a trainer before trying resistance exercises, since these may be more stressful for arthritic joints.

Water workouts. Aquatic activities aren't just for aerobic workouts. They're also a great strength training option for those with OA because water provides natural resistance and is gentle on the joints, too. (See page 32 for more information.)

A full-body strength training program should take about 20 to 30 minutes to complete. The American College of Sports Medicine recommends at least one set of 8 to 12 reps for each exercise for people under age 50, while people age 50 and older should use lighter weights that allow 10 to 15 reps. The number of times you perform each rep is called a set: For example, 8 biceps curls followed by a few minutes of rest is considered one set. If you're short on time, try to do at least one set of exercises for your shoulders, chest, abdomen, back, buttocks, and legs. Remember, something is always better than nothing.

Stretching and Flexibility (Daily)

It's no secret that regular stretching can make can you more limber and loose. You don't need to be as bendable as Gumby, but by being more flexible, you'll be able to move stiff joints more easily. Another benefit of flexibility is that it can lead to more-stable muscles and joints, which can keep you from taking a spill if painful knees or hips make walking difficult. Plus, the relaxation you'll feel when stretching can counteract stress, which can make achy joints feel even more painful. Your physical therapist or a fitness instructor may show you some simple stretches to perform every day, or you might try yoga or tai chi, two ancient Eastern disciplines that help to promote flexibility.

Tai chi. Have you ever noticed people in your local park or fitness center performing a series of slow, flowing, smoothly linked arm and leg motions? They're probably practicing tai chi, a gentle Asian martial art designed to harmonize the circulation of energy (*chi*) around the body. Tai chi is often practiced outside, and its movements tend to have elegant names, such as Waving Hands in the Clouds and White Crane Spreads His Wings.

It might sound strange, but many people—including those with OA—who regularly practice tai chi say that the exercises make them feel better both physically and mentally. For example, research shows that people with OA who practice tai chi in a twice-weekly, hour-long class say that they're more flexible, move more easily, and have less trouble bending and doing household tasks. What's more, studies have also found that tai chi has a wide range of other health benefits, such as improving muscle strength, flexibility, range of motion, balance, and mood; reducing the risk of hip fractures in the elderly; and even lowering blood pressure. Fortunately, experts say that almost anyone with OA can safely do tai chi. Even so, many tai chi movements involve bending the knees, so ask your instructor for more comfortable adaptations to those exercises if you have knee OA (many classes geared toward people with arthritis teach "Sun Style" tai chi, which is easier on the knee joints). To locate tai chi classes for people with arthritis, contact your local chapter of the Arthritis Foundation.

DR. WEIL SAYS: "Tai chi can ease stiffness and enhance the quality of life for those with osteoarthritis. While water exercise can also soothe osteoarthritis, tai chi does not require a pool. It's also easy to learn, suitable for all ages, and can be done safely by those with physical limitations."

Yoga. You don't need to twist yourself into a pretzel or stand on your head to reap the benefits of this ancient Hindu mind-body regimen. Yoga incorporates body postures (called *asanas*) with breathing exercises (*pranayama*) and meditation. In fact, practicing even simple yoga poses can help you relax, improve your flexibility, balance, and strength, and help stabilize your joints. Studies show that people with OA of the knee who regularly practice yoga have 50 percent less pain after just two months. In addition, other research shows that people who regularly practice a series of yogic hand exercises can significantly reduce OA pain in their fingers.

You'll want to try a few group or private yoga classes first, so you become familiar with how to do the basic postures safely. Some experts say that Iyengar yoga may be the best bet for people with OA, since it relies on blankets, pillows, blocks, and other props to help you do the poses correctly without straining yourself. But whatever type of yoga you try, tell the instructor that you have OA, so you can learn how to modify certain postures when necessary to reduce your risk of injury. When you can't make it to class, you can practice on your own using a book or yoga video geared specifically to people with arthritis (see Resource Guide for details).

Taking the Plunge with Warm Water Workouts

You don't need to live near the beach, own a pool, or even know how to swim to enjoy the many benefits of water exercise, but once you've given this activity a try, you'll be glad you got wet. The same warm water that makes it delightful to soak your achy joints in a bathtub or whirlpool can also do wonders for them when you move gently around a heated pool. When you do an aquatic workout, make sure the water temperature is warm—between 83 and 88 degrees—since this will relax your muscles and ease joint stiffness. Another advantage of exercising in warm water is that you can get a full-body workout that may incorporate an aerobic component, stretching and flexibility, as well as strength training.

In all likelihood, you'll probably start with a water-exercise class geared toward people with OA and other types of arthritis. In such classes, you'll perform simple movements (like flicking your fingers, bending your knees, rotating your hips, and moving your ankles in circles) that may feel painful on land but are therapeutic in the water. As anyone who's floated on their back or treaded water knows, water supports your body weight, which means less strain on your hips, knees, and spine. In fact, the buoyancy of water reduces the weight your joints normally bear on land by up to 90 percent. So it's no surprise that water exercise is incredibly soothing for people with OA: Activity that might be otherwise uncomfortable can become a joy in the water, where your body floats easily and almost defies gravity. Even better, you don't need to know how to swim, since shallow-water activity takes place in water no more than chest-high, and deeper water exercises rely on floatation devices. Arthritis water workout classes may also foster a sense of camaraderie and even act as a support group, since you'll meet others who have OA.

You'll find a wide variety of other water-exercise programs offered at YMCAs and fitness centers—everything from walking in water that's knee- to shoulder-high to gentle stretching and water aerobics. Some clubs even offer water cycling and water yoga. To dress the part, you'll need a comfortable

Sticking with It: Making Exercise Work for You

You might have to force yourself to exercise when first starting out, especially if achy joints keep you glued to the couch. But if you can stick with it for a few weeks, it's likely to become a habit—and an enjoyable one at that. In fact, people with OA who regularly exercise say they don't feel the same when they miss a day. If that's not enough incentive, ask a friend to join you and become your exercise buddy: Research suggests that exercising with others doubles your chances of keeping at it. Another possibility is to establish an unthinking routine, such as exercising first thing in the morning before you're really awake and can talk yourself out of it. Pack your gym bag the night before, so you can get up and go. Or try giving yourself (nonfood) rewards for meeting your fitness goals, like a massage after you walk your first mile or a new CD when you attend four weekly water-arthritis classes.

Exercise need not be drudgery. Exercising outdoors in interesting surroundings makes the time pass more quickly. If you prefer to work out indoors, spice up your routine by doing it to music or listening to books on tape. To prevent boredom, vary your activity from day to day, an approach known as cross training. For example, do a water workout one day, a tai chi class another, and use an elliptical trainer the next. Or invest in a pedometer. This small, relatively inexpensive gadget counts each step you take, which can inspire you to do more walking. And don't miss out on opportunities to lead a more active, less sedentary life every day: taking a walk with your friends rather than sitting and talking, working in your garden, dancing around your living room. After all, every little bit counts.

bathing suit, a swim cap, goggles (if you swim), and possibly a pair of aqua shoes. This special footwear gives you traction and keeps your feet free of the small scrapes you could get from the bottom of the pool.

You can comfortably do aerobic exercises (including walking) in a pool, since the warm water surrounding you soothes tense muscles and cushions your joints. Plus, exercising in water can maximize your workout: Walking on land burns about 135 calories in a half-hour, while walking in deep water burns almost twice that many.

Working out in water provides resistance for strength training, too. Because water offers at least 12 times more resistance than air, simple movements like pushing water away from and pulling it toward you with your hands, using special water weights, or wearing water-workout gear like hand mitts and fins can all give you as good a workout as on land, and perhaps a better one.

Resources. To locate a water-exercise program designed for people with arthritis, or to order a free brochure on water exercise, contact your local office of the Arthritis Foundation.

CHAPTER FOUR

Managing Pain with Mind-Body Measures

Just as exercising can strengthen your body, you can draw on the power of your mind to make it easier to contend with OA. Treatment efforts for OA that focus only on your body's physical symptoms—and neglect the condition's impact on your mind and emotions—are missing out on some valuable ways to lessen pain, enhance mental outlook, and improve quality of life. That's because your mind is a powerful tool that can be harnessed to help influence your body and promote healing. The best way to do this is to practice a mind-body technique.

Although conventional medicine tends to ignore the link between the mind and the body, the effect of your emotions on your physical health is quite clear. There's no question that stress can affect how you feel, both emotionally and physically. When you're feeling worried, anxious, or depressed, your body's sympathetic nervous system pumps out stress hormones like cortisol and adrenaline, which increase heart rate, blood pressure, and muscle tension. These stress hormones also work to lower your body's pain threshold, making weak, achy joints feel even more painful. In addition, you'll find yourself breathing more rapidly and shallowly when you're stressed.

> "A strong positive mental attitude will create more miracles than any wonder drug."
>
> PATRICIA NEAL

DR. WEIL SAYS: "I remember once interviewing a patient from New York City, and I asked her, 'Do you have any particular stress in your life?' She said, 'Life is stressful.' I have to agree with her. I think it's impossible to live without stress. What we *can* do is learn how to neutralize stress and protect our bodies from its many harmful influences."

Clearly, emotional stress triggers a reaction in your body, and yet the reverse is also true: Physical pain can also affect you emotionally. When you're constantly in pain, it can make you feel sad, angry, or moody. Achy joints can also make it difficult to complete your daily chores, do your job efficiently, or spend time with friends. What's more, OA-related pain may make it hard for you to sleep, which can make you irritable and unable to concentrate. The more pain limits your activities, the more likely you'll feel frustrated and dependent on others. All this can make it easy for people with OA to feel depressed (see box on page 39 for more).

With so much interplay between the mind and body, especially when it comes to pain, measures that influence both your physical and mental health have to be an important part of an integrative approach to treating OA. Mind-body therapies assume that your thoughts, attitudes, beliefs, and emotions all influence your physical health and well-being. By learning how to focus your attention through mind-body techniques, you can not only achieve a more relaxed state of mind, you can also affect your physiology, taking the edge off pain and other arthritis-related symptoms. When you discover how to lower your level of stress, you may notice that painful joints don't seem to hurt as much. That's because stress reduction techniques like mind-body approaches can help you become aware of shallow breathing, muscle tension, and other contributors to pain and anxiety. When you regularly practice breath work, meditation, or self-hypnosis, you'll learn to concentrate on making your breathing slow and deep, and focus less on feelings of pain and worry and intrusive thoughts. Plus, you'll feel more relaxed and tend to notice pain less.

The Most Effective Mind–Body Measures

While not every mind-body approach discussed here has been studied for its effect on OA, many have been shown to greatly improve the quality of life for people with physical illness in general and may enhance your body's ability to heal itself. For example, you can use guided imagery techniques to envision healing in your arthritic joints. You can use meditation to help slow down your breathing and quiet your mind—if only for the duration of the exercise—and shift your concentration away from your everyday worries. You may even be able to lower your dose of pain medications by practicing a mind-body technique, although you probably won't be able to stop taking drugs altogether. Still, these approaches are valuable tools for managing painful joints, boosting your immune system, and coping with other health problems you may have. Even better, they're unlikely to cause harm, generally don't take much time to practice, and are relatively inexpensive—three good reasons to give them a try. Once you are taught how to do some of these mind-body techniques correctly, you can practice them whenever or wherever you like or need them, although some approaches may require that you work only with a trained practitioner. Choose one or more of the mind-body techniques that most appeal to you and practice it daily.

> **DR. WEIL SAYS:** "I recommend regularly practicing a relaxation technique, such as breath work, meditation, or a course of biofeedback, all of which can help modify your perception of OA pain."

Biofeedback. Compared to most mind-body therapies—which rely mainly on using your emotions to influence your body—biofeedback is decidedly high-tech. This painless, noninvasive therapy uses electronic devices to measure a host of biological functions, including heart rate, muscle tension, blood pressure, and body temperature. This equipment then "feeds" this information back to patients so they can learn to regulate these functions through relaxation, imagery, and other techniques.

HOW IT HELPS ▶ Biofeedback hasn't been studied for OA, but practitioners

Seeking Support for Osteoarthritis

Chronic OA pain can hurt so much that you may not feel up to socializing with friends and family. And no matter how much your loved ones may try to help, you've probably wondered if they really understand the pain you're feeling on a daily basis. But it's important to get emotional support from others who will listen to your concerns, discuss your abilities and limitations, and simply offer a sympathetic ear when you need it most. After all, confiding your worries is a great first step in taking control of your OA and changing your outlook on living with the condition.

When seeking support, look to your family and close friends first (see page 63 for more on OA and your relationships). In addition, support groups and self-help programs have also been shown to improve mood and reduce participants' need for pain medication.

One good choice for support is the Arthritis Foundation's Arthritis Self-Help Course (ASHC), a group education program meant to complement the professional services provided by your health-care team. Trained volunteers, many of whom have arthritis themselves,

lead the courses, which are designed to identify and teach you the latest pain management techniques, help you find solutions to problems caused by your OA, discover ways to deal with anger, fear, frustration, and depression, learn new ways to communicate with family and friends, and much more. The course allows you to share experiences with others in the same situation, offering you the opportunity to both help and learn from people like yourself. (For more information, contact your local Arthritis Foundation chapter.)

Try This: The Relaxing Breath

Lots of people find that Dr. Weil's yoga-derived Relaxing Breath is one of the most effective and time-efficient relaxation methods out there. Try it for yourself and see if this breathing exercise produces a pleasant altered state and helps relieve OA-related pain and tension.

1 Sit or lie comfortably

with your back straight, and place your tongue in what's called the yogic position: Touch the tip of your tongue to the back of your upper front teeth and slide it up until it rests on the ridge of tissue between your teeth and palate. Keep your tongue there for the duration of the exercise.

2 Exhale completely

and loudly through your mouth.

3 Close your mouth lightly

and inhale through your nose quietly to the count of 4.

4 Hold your breath

for a count of 7.

5 Exhale audibly

through your mouth to the count of 8. If you have difficulty exhaling with your tongue in place, try pursing your lips.

Repeat steps 3 through 5

three more times, for a total of four cycles. Breathe normally and observe how your body feels.

The key to doing this exercise is keeping to the ratio of 4:7:8, ensuring that your exhalation is twice as long as your inhalation. It doesn't matter how fast or slow you count; your pace will be determined by how long you can comfortably hold your breath.

Practice this exercise at least twice a day, preferably when you first wake up and before you go to sleep, or just before meditating. After a month of practice, you can increase the number of breath cycles to eight. This exercise is safe for everyone, although people with chronic obstructive pulmonary disease (COPD) or other respiratory problems may not wish to hold their breath for too long while doing it; just count at a pace that feels comfortable to you while maintaining the 4:7:8 ratio.

say it can help to relax muscles, which may help relieve joint pain.

GETTING STARTED ▶ A biofeedback session begins with painless sensors being attached to your body. Next, the practitioner will teach you mental imagery techniques which, when practiced correctly, can help you control your body temperature, heart rate, muscle tension, or other functions. With OA, for example, you may be asked to envision your muscles becoming soft and loose, while an electronic device helps you to be aware of the level of tension. You'll probably need several sessions of biofeedback to see results.

RESOURCES ▶ For a qualified biofeedback practitioner, send a SASE to the Biofeedback Certification Institute of America, *10200 W. 44th Ave., #310, Wheat Ridge CO 80033*, or visit *www.bcia.org*.

Breath work. Breathing seems pretty straightforward: You inhale and exhale, and you probably don't think you need an instruction manual. But, in truth, most people *don't* breathe properly, taking short, fast, shallow breaths rather than taking full advantage of their respiratory system. To breathe more effectively and optimize the power of your lungs and other respiratory organs, you'll want to regularly practice breathing more slowly and deeply. By doing so, you'll learn how breath work can reduce stress, benefiting a number of health conditions, including the chronic pain caused by OA.

HOW IT HELPS ▶ You may find that regularly practicing breathing exercises like those described here increases blood circulation throughout your body, nourishing your achy joints by supplying them with more oxygen and nutrients. Deep breathing also decreases anxiety and improves your sleep and your energy levels, among many other benefits.

GETTING STARTED ▶ The most subtle and powerful form of breath work is also the simplest: Just follow your breath. Sit or lie comfortably with your spine straight, close your eyes, and focus your attention on your breathing, without trying to influence it in any way. You'll notice that following your breath is pleasant and relaxing, a way of putting your mind and body in "neutral." If your mind starts to wander, just gently bring it back to your breathing. Practice this simple meditation five minutes each day. You'll also want try to make your breathing slow, deep, quiet, and regular, which can deliver more oxygen to your arthritic joints.

RESOURCES ▶ For more, check out Dr. Weil's recording *Breathing: The Master Key to Self Healing*. (To order, call *888-337-9345*.)

Recognizing Depression

Studies show that up to one-fifth of people with OA also suffer from clinical depression. That's not surprising, since the pain and frustration you experience with OA may trigger depression. What's more, some people with OA may be naturally predisposed to clinical depression, and living with the painful, stiff joints caused by OA exacerbates this mental health condition.

Not sure if you're depressed? Remember that clinical depression is much more than having the blues or simply feeling sad. A diagnosis of depression (which can range from mild to severe) requires feelings of sadness or grief or loss of interest in everyday activities for at least two weeks, plus at least four of the following symptoms: a change in appetite or weight, an inability to sleep or oversleeping, restlessness, reduced energy, difficulty concentrating or making decisions, feelings of guilt or worthlessness, or thoughts of death or suicide. These symptoms must be severe enough to interfere with your ability to function daily (working, interacting with friends and family, etc.). If you feel that you may be depressed, see your doctor, who can refer you to a mental health professional and discuss medications and lifestyle measures that may help you feel better.

DR. WEIL SAYS: "My personal favorite stress reduction technique is breath work. Breath is a very powerful connection between the mind and the body. Breath is unique in our physiological functions in that it's the only thing you can control either completely voluntarily or completely involuntarily."

Guided imagery. In this safe, time- and cost-effective—and often fun—technique, you'll use mental imagery suggested by books, audiotapes, or a trained practitioner to relieve stress and envision your body healing itself. For instance, someone seeking relaxation might be asked to picture a day at the beach, while someone with OA might imagine breathing into the pain and having each exhalation ease it slightly.

HOW IT HELPS ▶ Research has shown that the same parts of your brain become active whether you imagine something or actually experience it. This means that picturing your body healing itself—your arthritic joints becoming healthy again—may actually result in less OA pain and other symptoms. Although research on guided imagery and OA still needs to be done, this

Try This: Talking to Your Symptoms

This guided-imagery exercise from Martin Rossman, MD, can help you better understand the emotional meaning of your osteoarthritis symptoms. Although having a "dialogue" with your symptoms may feel strange at first, you may be surprised by what you learn from this intriguing exercise.

1 Relax. Close your eyes, take a few deep breaths, and then direct your attention to the symptom.

2 Observe. Allow an image to appear that represents this symptom. Accept whatever image comes, and observe it in detail. Notice any feelings that come up.

3 Communicate. Now tell the image how you feel about it, silently or out loud.

- Give the image a voice, and let it answer you. Ask the image why it's there, what it wants from you, what it needs from you, and what it's trying to do for you.

- Ask the image if it's willing to give you any relief from your symptom if you're willing to give it what it wants or needs. If so, continue to dialogue until you've made a bargain.

When you feel done, gradually bring yourself back to the everyday world, and write down anything important from your experience.

Try This: Progressive Muscle Relaxation

You can help ease joint and muscle pain by relieving stress muscle-by-muscle with this simple technique, known as progressive muscle relaxation (PMR). Try this exercise sitting or lying down in a quiet place, whichever feels most comfortable.

- Close your eyes and concentrate on your breathing for a few seconds. Now focus on a single body part or muscle group, say, your right foot.

- While taking a deep inhaling breath, tense the muscles in your right foot—not to the point of pain—and hold for 3 to 5 seconds.

- Then slowly relax the foot as you exhale and let stress flow from your body. Pause for a few seconds.

- Continue this tense and release sequence as you move up the right leg to the calves and thighs, then to the left foot, and gradually to the buttocks, abdomen, each arm, shoulders, and face.

- Finally, scan the body for any unresolved areas of tension.

- Practice for 10 to 15 minutes each day, or when time is limited, try a shortened version by doing the lower body, upper body, and face.

approach is currently used in many health-care settings as an adjunctive therapy for chronic pain in general.

GETTING STARTED ▸ Ideally, you may be able to help overcome or control OA pain by visualizing the anatomical details of healing. Ask your doctor to explain the arthritic process—and how healing might occur—in terms you can understand and visualize. For example, you might imagine worn, dry cartilage becoming moist and spongy again. Practice your healing imagery for a few minutes at least twice a day, and see what it does for you. Keep in mind that it may take several weeks of regular practice to see benefits.

RESOURCES ▸ To locate a practitioner, contact the Academy for Guided Imagery at *www.interactiveimagery.com* or *(800) 726-2070*. Two helpful books on the topic are *Guided Imagery for Self-Healing* (second edition) by Martin Rossman, MD (HJ Kramer, 2000), and *Staying Well with Guided Imagery* by Belleruth Naparstek (Warner, 1995). Both authors have also produced excellent guided-imagery audiotapes: Naparstek's are available from Image Paths at *www.healthjourneys.com* or *(800) 800-8661* and Rossman's are available from the Academy for Guided Imagery. Another recent recording to try is *Self-Healing with Guided Imagery*, in which Dr. Weil and Dr. Rossman team up to introduce you to this mind-body practice. To order, call *(888) 337-9345*.

Hypnotherapy. Known as "sleep healing" in ancient Greece and "mind cure" in the fourteenth through mid-nineteenth centuries, what we now call hypnosis has a long history of therapeutic use. Essentially, a trance is an altered state of consciousness that you deliberately choose to enter to help focus your concentration and use suggestion to promote healing.

HOW IT HELPS ▶ Hypnotherapy hasn't yet been studied specifically for OA, but it's currently being used at the University of Arizona's Integrative Medicine Clinic to effectively treat a remarkable range of related conditions, including chronic pain and anxiety and sleep disorders.

GETTING STARTED ▶ Typically, a clinical hypnotherapist will teach you some type of "induction technique"—the use of a focal point, either internal or external, to concentrate your attention (Hollywood's version is the swinging pendant). Once you're in a state of trance (but still fully aware of where you are and what you're doing), the therapist will offer suggestions specifically geared to the goal of the therapy. For example, he may suggest that a person with an arthritic knee imagine moving the joint without feeling stiffness and

Try This: Self-Hypnosis

This self-hypnosis exercise comes from Steven Gurgevich, PhD, a mind-body medicine specialist at the University of Arizona's Program in Integrative Medicine. You can practice it whenever you like to help relax your mind and body, possibly relieving OA pain.

- Sit comfortably. With your eyes open, gaze up as high as you can. Now take a deep breath. As you exhale, gently close your eyes, and let your eyes rest in any position they prefer. Leisurely scan your body (starting with the head and moving downward), thinking or imagining that each body part is relaxing and releasing tension.

- Upon reaching your toes, allow your body to rest where it is, as you imagine going to a "special place." It could be a beach with gentle waves, a fragrant spring meadow, or anywhere you've felt calm and content. Imagine being there now, and all the colors, shapes, sounds, smells, tastes, and textures of this place.

- Now count down from 10 to 0, imagining that with each number you're going deeper into this setting and that your body and mind are relaxing more deeply. After you're done counting, repeat to yourself, "I am calm, I am relaxed, I am at peace," for as long as you wish.

- When you're ready to return, gradually bring your attention back to your body, open your eyes, and enjoy feeling peaceful and refreshed.

Try This: Meditation

A mantra is a meaningful word or phrase that you repeat during meditation, either silently or out loud. You can choose a holy name or brief prayer from your religious tradition, or you can choose a neutral word or phrase such as "One," "Peace," or "Let go." First, assume a comfortable position and gently close your eyes. Take a few deep breaths. Then let your breath come naturally and begin to repeat your mantra at whatever rhythm feels comfortable to you. If your mind begins to wander, gently bring it back to your mantra. Try this simple meditation for at least a few minutes and see if you notice less pain.

pain. Your unconscious mind can then transmit these thoughts and images throughout your mind and body, setting the healing process in motion. A typical course of hypnotherapy may require from one to five visits (lasting 45 minutes to an hour each), depending on your hypnotizability, the medical condition involved, and your response to treatment. (Your health insurance plan may cover this if it's performed by an MD, a PhD, or a licensed social worker.) Remember, the therapist's role is to teach you how to access the trance state on your own. Once you've learned how to do this, you can start using self-hypnosis on a regular basis to maximize your healing potential.

RESOURCES ▶ For a list of qualified practitioners near you, send a SASE along with a request indicating your state and city to the American Society of Clinical Hypnosis, *140 N. Bloomingdale Rd., Bloomingdale IL 60108.* For more information on hypnotherapy, check out Dr. Steven Gurgevich's website at *www.tranceformation.com.*

Meditation. In its most basic sense, meditation is simply directed concentration. You'll learn to focus your awareness and direct it onto an object: the breath, a repeated word or phrase (known as a mantra), or a mental image. By keeping your attention in one place, you're also removing your focus from anxious thoughts and the mental chatter that can often fill your head. Meditation quiets your mind and can offer a sense of balance and centeredness when you're feeling stressed, whether it's from juggling a busy schedule or coping with a chronic condition like OA.

HOW IT HELPS ▶ Meditation hasn't been researched for OA in particular, but studies have demonstrated that when done regularly, it can help improve chronic pain, and this approach is now an accepted mind-body therapy used at hundreds of clinics and hospitals. Still, meditation isn't for everyone: Some people need relaxation techniques that give faster results, such as the Relaxing

Breath exercise (see page 38). Others have trouble sitting still and might prefer mindful forms of movement, such as yoga or tai chi. It may not be a good idea for people who are mentally ill to meditate without supervision.

GETTING STARTED ▶ You'll want to choose a quiet place—inside or outside—where you won't be interrupted, and find a comfortable position, sitting if possible (you don't have to sit in the cross-legged lotus position). While meditating, if your mind begins to wander, gently bring it back to your breath or your chosen object of meditation. Of course, the tricky part of meditation is this constant running after your attention and bringing it back to a more focused place. But be patient: As your meditation practice deepens, your mental concentration will become more focused. Try to meditate every day, beginning with five minutes a day and slowly working up to 15 or 20 minutes once or twice a day. If you can't do a full session, try to fit in a few minutes at some point during your day. Also, don't meditate after a big meal, which can make you drowsy. How do you know if your meditation is "paying off"? You'll probably gradually notice subtle changes in your daily life, such as feeling less reactive and being more patient with others, or feeling more open, more aware, and more in control of your life.

RESOURCES ▶ Some good books for beginners are *How to Meditate* by Lawrence LeShan, PhD (Little, Brown, 1999), and *Wherever You Go, There You Are* by Jon Kabat-Zinn, PhD (Hyperion, 1995). You might also try listening to the recording *Meditation for Optimum Health*, which includes meditation exercises led by Drs. Kabat-Zinn and Weil. (To order, call *888-337-9345*.)

CHAPTER FIVE

Experimenting with Alternative Approaches

Being told you may need to take pain medication for the rest of your life to treat OA can be extremely discouraging. While NSAIDs and other drugs can relieve the pain and stiffness in your joints, you might be concerned about the potential side effects of these medications, especially when you may need to stay on them for years. Some people simply don't like the idea of taking a drug and feeling dependent on it to lessen pain. So it's no wonder that many people with OA turn to alternative therapies to help themselves feel better.

Although the following modalities won't necessarily eliminate your need for pain medication, regularly using one or more of them may reduce the number or dosage of OA drugs you take, and give you a sense of control over your pain. These therapies can be an important part of an OA-relief program that also includes exercising regularly, eating a wholesome diet, maintaining a healthy weight, and practicing mind-body approaches. Here are some of the more promising alternative therapies for OA. While not all of them have been studied specifically for OA, they offer hope for decreasing chronic pain, easing symptoms, relieving stress, and improving your general sense of well-being.

Acupuncture. This ancient healing art is an integral part of the comprehensive healing system of traditional Chinese medicine, which holds that an imbalance of the body's energy flow (called *chi*) can cause disease. A practitioner will determine where the energy blockages are in your body and what points along your meridians (energy channels) to stimulate with needles in order to correct this imbalance.

HOW IT HELPS ▶ Acupuncture is a promising treatment for OA. In fact,

> "Medicine is not only a science; it is also an art."
>
> PARACELSUS

Try This: Acupressure for Pain Relief

This do-it-yourself healing technique does not use needles, but aims to stimulate the same acupuncture points on the body to relieve arthritis pain temporarily. Try pressing on acupressure point LI4, in the webbed space between the thumb and index finger, to relieve arthritic pain in the hands, wrists, and shoulders. To ease knee OA, press on point ST36, about four finger-widths below the kneecap. For either point, press firmly with your index finger or thumb for 30 seconds until you feel a dull ache, then continue pressing down for another 30 to 60 seconds.

positive results from a small study on the use of acupuncture to relieve pain and improve function in patients with knee OA have prompted a larger trial of this technique. In this study, acupuncture was found effective when done in addition to taking anti-inflammatory medications. So if you have regular acupuncture sessions, you may be able to reduce your drug dosage.

GETTING STARTED▶ During a typical session, an acupuncturist will insert needles into different parts of your body as you lie on a table. In many cases, you won't even feel the needle going in; in other cases, you may feel a slight tingling or burning. The needles are typically left in for 10 to 20 minutes. An initial assessment and treatment can run anywhere between an hour and two hours, with follow-up sessions generally lasting between 45 minutes and an hour. In all, you may need some 4 to 10 acupuncture sessions, scheduled once or twice a week, and will then probably be put on a maintenance regimen of monthly treatments for another three months or so.

RESOURCES▶ To find a practitioner near you, contact the National Certification Commission for Acupuncture and Oriental Medicine (NCCAOM) at *www.nccaom.org* or *(703) 548-9004*; the American Academy of Medical Acupuncture (MDs only) at *www.medicalacupuncture.org* or *(323) 937-5514*; or the National Acupuncture and Oriental Medicine Alliance (an umbrella organization that includes both Chinese-medicine practitioners and MDs) at *www.aomalliance.org* or *(253) 851-6896*.

Alexander Technique. In this form of movement education, practitioners guide clients through simple movements, teaching them how to reduce muscle tension and restore the body's natural poise. The goal of the Alexander Technique is proper alignment of your head, neck, and spine, which will allow your body to move more efficiently.

HOW IT HELPS▶ Although the Alexander Technique hasn't yet been researched for OA, practitioners of the approach report that it can benefit people with OA and other chronic pain conditions by helping them improve their posture and learn to move in new ways that cause less pain.

GETTING STARTED ▶ You'll remain fully clothed and lie on a padded bodywork table during part of the session while the practitioner gently moves your head and limbs to release areas of muscular tension. Also, the practitioner will observe how you sit, stand, and walk, and will use verbal instructions and light touch to re-educate you on how to perform these everyday functions more comfortably. If you're like most people, you'll feel taller after a session, due to the lengthening of your spine achieved by this technique.

RESOURCES ▶ To locate a practitioner, contact the American Society of the Alexander Technique at *www.alexandertech.org* or *(800) 473-0620.*

Chiropractic. Practitioners of this hands-on modality are most concerned with the relationship between your body's structure (primarily the spine) and its function (primarily of the nervous system). Actually, the mainstay of chiropractic treatment is the correction of so-called subluxations (misalignments of the spine) through the use of spinal manipulation (called spinal adjustments).

HOW IT HELPS ▶ While more light still needs to be shed on the benefits of chiropractic care, some case reports from chiropractors suggest that this therapy may improve pain and the ability to move easily in people with OA.

GETTING STARTED ▶ First, your chiropractor will take a case history, a basic physical exam, an examination of your spine, joints, and muscles, and other tests. Once your complaint has been identified and treatment approaches discussed, you may receive spinal adjustments on a special mechanized table. Typically, after preparation and positioning, the chiropractor will apply pressure to the relevant joint to return it to its proper position. Don't be surprised if you hear a popping sound similar to the one you make when you crack your knuckles, which is caused by the sudden release of built-up pressure in the joint and which should be painless. In addition to adjustments, many chiropractors offer other treatment methods as well, such as soft-tissue manipulation, trigger-point therapy, physical therapy, nutritional counseling, and even acupuncture. (*Note*: Chiropractic may not be a good idea for people with serious bone problems, such as osteoporosis, bone or joint infections, bone cancer, acute rheumatoid arthritis, and diseases of the spinal cord or bone marrow.)

RESOURCES ▶ For more information, contact the American Chiropractic Association at *www.amerchiro.org* or *(800) 986-4636.*

Feldenkrais Method. Like the Alexander Technique, this approach uses subtle movements to retrain your nervous system, to help it find new pathways around areas of pain or damage. A Feldenkrais practitioner will guide you in breaking down movement patterns to re-educate your brain and nervous system to change patterns of movement that may be linked with pain. Through repetition, you'll experience new, more-efficient ways of moving as normal.

HOW IT HELPS ▶ The Feldenkrais Method isn't well studied for OA, but some people whose movement has been restricted by OA find that it can greatly improve their range of motion and flexibility.

GETTING STARTED ▶ You've got two options for learning Feldenkrais: group classes or individual instruction. Most people do both. In "Awareness Through Movement" group classes, a practitioner uses verbal instructions to guide you through simple floor exercises that involve common movements like bending, turning, leaning, and breathing to help each student discover the ways he or she moves most easily. Alternatively, you could try a private "Functional Integration" session, in which the practitioner offers gentle hands-on guidance in performing movements tailored to your particular health condition. In both the group classes and private sessions, you'll remain fully clothed.

RESOURCES ▶ To locate a practitioner, contact the Feldenkrais Guild of North America at *www.feldenkrais.com* or *(800) 775-2118.*

Massage. This hands-on manipulation of muscles and soft tissues comes in many different forms, which can all promote relaxation and ease tension.

HOW IT HELPS ▶ Massage may benefit people with OA by encouraging blood flow to stiff joints. And it may relieve pain by lowering levels of stress hormones and boosting endorphins, your body's natural painkillers.

GETTING STARTED ▶ Before the massage begins, you may be asked to remove as much clothing as you're comfortable with and given a sheet, towel, or gown to drape over you while lying or sitting on a specially padded table or chair. In many forms of massage, oil is applied to your skin. Be sure to tell the practitioner if there are parts of your body that you don't want worked on, or whether or not you want to talk during the massage. Once the massage begins, you can make it more enjoyable by taking deep, relaxing breaths and giving the practitioner feedback (let him know, for example, if you feel any discomfort). Some health insurers may cover massage therapy—especially if you are referred by your physician—but check first with your own plan.

RESOURCES ▶ For more information, contact the American Massage Therapy Association at *www.amtamassage.org* or *(847) 864-0123.*

TENS. Transcutaneous electrical nerve stimulation (TENS) uses electrical impulses transmitted by a small machine and then sent through electrodes placed on or near sore areas to stimulate nerve endings, temporarily relieving joint pain. You'll find that physical therapists often use TENS or a related therapy—percutaneous electrical nerve stimulation (PENS), which relies on electrical impulses sent through acupuncture-type needles (rather than electrodes) inserted *into* the skin to stimulate nerves. Because TENS machines are small and portable, you can use them on your own at home.

HOW IT HELPS ▸ It's unclear exactly how TENS helps alleviate pain, but researchers believe that the electrical stimulation of the nerve endings may block pain sensations relayed to the brain and trigger the release of endorphins, chemicals that act as natural painkillers. In fact, one analysis of seven previous studies of TENS found that the therapy worked better than a placebo treatment at relieving pain in people with OA of the knee.

GETTING STARTED ▸ Your first experience with TENS may be during physical therapy, where electrodes will be placed on your skin near painful joints. These electrodes are connected to a TENS machine—a small, battery-operated unit—whose electrical intensity can be adjusted until you feel a prickling or tingling, but not painful, sensation where the electrodes meet the skin. The procedure will take anywhere from 30 minutes to an hour, and relieves joint pain for a few hours after it ends. Since a TENS machine is only about as big as a cell phone, you can also purchase one from medical supply retailers or borrow it from your physical therapist for at-home use.

RESOURCES ▸ Ask your physician or physical therapist about TENS, or see websites like *www.tens-store.com* for information on purchasing a machine (which may cost between $50 and $100).

Therapeutic Touch. This therapy's name is something of a misnomer, since it rarely involves actual touch. Instead, practitioners (mostly registered nurses) use their hands to assess and balance the energy field surrounding your body in order to promote your own natural ability to heal.

HOW IT HELPS ▸ Some research shows that people with OA of the knee who receive weekly Therapeutic Touch (TT) sessions report less pain, a higher level of function, and greater well-being than those who do not.

GETTING STARTED ▸ During a session of TT, you'll remain fully clothed and may sit in a chair, but you can lie down if sitting is uncomfortable. The practitioner moves her hands a few inches above your body, from head to toe, to sense areas of imbalance in your personal energy field. The practitioner then "unruffles" areas of congested energy with a series of sweeping hand movements and, finally, transmits energy to deficient areas by holding her hands above them. You can expect to feel relaxed and energized by TT treatments.

RESOURCES ▶ See *A Doctor's Guide to Therapeutic Touch* by Susan Wager, MD (Perigee, 1996). To locate a practitioner, contact Nurse Healers-Professional Associates International at *www.therapeutic-touch.org* or *(801) 273-3399.*

What About ...

Copper bracelets. This home remedy for arthritis has been around since the time of the ancient Greeks, yet little research has been done to support its use. Proponents claim that arthritis is the result of a copper deficiency and so wearing a copper bracelet on your arm will alleviate the condition because you'll absorb this metal through your skin. Copper is an important micronutrient, but you can meet your needs (about 2 mg per day) through food or a multivitamin. So far, only one poorly designed study has shown reduced pain in arthritis sufferers who wore the bracelets; another, larger study showed no effect.

Magnet therapy. Just a few small, short-term studies have been done on the possible pain-reducing benefits of low-intensity static (non-electrified) magnets, and they have produced conflicting results. Yet, many people say that they have found pain relief from magnetic skin patches, shoe inserts, splints, and even mattress pads. As long as you're not pregnant or do not use a pacemaker or implanted defibrillator, it's okay to use small magnets for pain relief if you find them helpful. But keep in mind that so far we have no idea whether they're safe for long-term use or exactly how they may work to lessen pain.

Prolotherapy. Short for "proliferative injection therapy," this treatment involves injecting a sugar-water solution, often mixed with a local anesthetic and sometimes other substances, into ligaments and tendons. The solution acts as an irritant, causing a mild inflammatory response. It might seem counterintuitive, but this process helps to stimulate your body's own healing system to lay down new ligament and tendon, stabilizing nearby joints. While prolotherapy needs more study, some research suggests that it can reduce joint pain and swelling in people with knee OA. If you try prolotherapy (typically administered by an MD or osteopathic physician), keep in mind that it may take several sessions to experience relief and that health insurance generally doesn't cover this treatment.

CHAPTER SIX

Choosing Supplements for Osteoarthritis

D ietary supplements can seem appealing if you're concerned about the potential side effects of OA pain medications or are simply curious about trying less toxic remedies. After all, supplements are "natural" and free of side effects, right? Not always. It's true that most supplements, which include vitamins, minerals, herbs, and other natural remedies, are less potent than conventional drugs and tend to pose less risk of toxicity. But that doesn't mean all supplements are safe, or even helpful.

In this chapter, you'll find some of the most popular supplements for OA. Those marked with a star ★ are Dr. Weil's top picks, while those with a check mark ✔ may also be worth trying (the others aren't generally helpful for OA). The supplements discussed here aren't likely to replace your conventional OA drugs altogether, but taking one or more of them regularly may help you cut back on your dose of pain medications (with your doctor's supervision). Remember, too, that supplements aren't a substitute for getting regular exercise, maintaining a healthy weight, reducing stress, and following the other lifestyle measures that are part of the comprehensive integrative treatment program for OA found in this book.

★ **Glucosamine and chondroitin sulfates.** These two supplements are synthetic versions of substances naturally produced by your body and found in healthy cartilage. Popularized by the 1997 book *The Arthritis Cure*, both substances have also been used for years by veterinarians to treat OA in dogs and horses. In test-tube studies, glucosamine has been shown to stimulate cartilage production, while chondroitin slows its removal, possibly helping prevent further joint injury and slowing the advancement of OA. According to

> "Nature does nothing uselessly."
>
> ARISTOTLE

a meta-analysis of 15 placebo-controlled studies on the effects of glucosamine sulfate and/or chondroitin sulfate on OA of the knee or hip, both compounds appear to help relieve pain and improve mobility in osteoarthritis patients (*Journal of the American Medical Association*, March 15, 2000).

HOW TO TAKE ▶ Just as with conventional medicine, your optimal doses of glucosamine and chondroitin are based on your weight. If you weigh less than 120 pounds, you should take a total of 1,000 mg a day of glucosamine and 800 mg of chondroitin. If you weigh more than 120 pounds, but less than 200, you'll need 1,500 mg a day of glucosamine and 1,200 mg of chondroitin. And people weighing more than 200 pounds should take 2,000 mg a day of glucosamine and 1,600 mg of chondroitin. However much you weigh, take these supplements in two or three divided doses throughout the day.

Glucosamine is available in several different forms, including glucosamine hydrochloride and glucosamine sulfate. It's unclear if one form is better than another, since it's the glucosamine itself that benefits OA, not the entire chemical compound. That being said, glucosamine sulfate has been better studied.

Because glucosamine and chondroitin work more slowly than medications, it may take at least two months to feel the full effects. Should you take one of these supplements without the other? A large multicenter trial is currently investigating this question to determine whether or not glucosamine and chondroitin taken together may be more effective than either one alone, but results won't be available for a few years. In the meantime, some people who are concerned about "mad cow disease" have avoided chondroitin, which is often derived from cow cartilage. But the safety risk posed by this supplement is probably minimal. Plus, neither supplement should be taken to *prevent* OA. (They won't harm you, but will likely do little good and will also have a deleterious effect on your wallet.)

POSSIBLE CONCERNS ▶ Since glucosamine is derived from crab, lobster, or shrimp shells, there's a small possibility it may cause an allergic reaction in people who are sensitive to shellfish. What's more, glucosamine may interact with certain diuretic drugs, while chondroitin may cause excessive bleeding if you're also taking the blood thinner heparin or even a daily aspirin. There's also been a theoretical concern, based on some small studies in animals, that glucosamine (an amino sugar) may affect insulin resistance, but a more recent study in humans found no such effect (*Archives of Internal Medicine*, July 13, 2003). Still, if you're a diabetic, it's a good idea to monitor your blood glucose levels more carefully when taking this supplement. There's not much published information to support the concern that these supplements could raise

"I frequently recommend glucosamine and chondroitin sulfates to my own patients and have seen good results. At this point, I feel these two supplements have a more proven track record than other natural remedies for OA."

cholesterol. If you've noticed this side effect, however, discontinue the remedy and see whether your cholesterol levels go down at your next doctor's visit.

★**Natural anti-inflammatories.** Herbs such as turmeric and ginger aren't just food seasonings: When these spices, along with the herb boswellia, are taken as supplements in higher doses, the anti-inflammatory compounds they contain may work as well as aspirin and ibuprofen for treating OA and other chronic pain conditions that involve inflammation. Indeed, many people with OA have had good results with natural anti-inflammatories. Research on the effect of ginger and other anti-inflammatory herbs on OA and other diseases is currently taking place at the Center for Phytomedicine Research at the University of Arizona, funded by the National Institutes of Health.

HOW TO TAKE ▶ For OA, your best bet may be a multiherb product like New Chapter's Zyflamend, which combines ginger, turmeric, and boswellia with other anti-inflammatory herbs, although it may take up to two months to see results. If you're already taking COX-2s or NSAIDs for OA pain and wish to switch to this herbal product, start on Zyflamend at half the recommended dose (on the product label) and continue taking your usual dose of conventional medication. After one month, cut the COX-2 or NSAID dose in half and increase the Zyflamend to the full recommended dose. A month later, take only the Zyflamend and see whether your symptoms stay at bay. You can find Zyflamend at health food stores (to find a retailer, visit *www.new-chapter.com*).

POSSIBLE CONCERNS ▶ Because ginger thins the blood, you should consult your physician before adding it to your regimen if you also take other blood-thinning herbs or medications (such as garlic, ginkgo, and especially Coumadin). It's also a good idea to stop supplementing with ginger a couple weeks before having surgery to prevent any bleeding problems.

✔**SAM-e.** Short for S-adenosylmethionine, this naturally occurring molecule delivers sulfur to your body's cartilage, where it helps build collagen bonds that make for strong joints. Actually, SAM-e has long been used to treat both OA and depression in Europe, where it's sold by prescription. And here in the United States, a review of 11 clinical studies on SAM-e and OA found that the supplement is more effective at improving joint pain than a placebo (dummy pill) and as effective as NSAIDs at improving joint function and reducing pain (*Journal of Family Practice*, May 2002).

HOW TO TAKE ▶ If you try SAM-e for OA, you'll want to start by taking 400 mg twice a day for two weeks, and then decreasing to a maintenance dose of 200 mg twice a day thereafter. Choose SAM-e products that are enteric-coated and labeled "butanedisulfonate," which is the supplement's more stable form.

POSSIBLE CONCERNS ▶ So far, SAM-e appears to lack the side effects of conventional NSAIDs, but may cause mild stomach upset, dry mouth, and insomnia in rare cases. In addition, SAM-e's breakdown in the body is believed to create molecules of homocysteine, a substance that may increase the risk of heart disease in high amounts. It's a good idea to supplement with vitamin B-complex—which lowers homocysteine levels—if you also take SAM-e. There don't appear to be any interactions between SAM-e and glucosamine/chondroitin supplements, but you'll likely only need to take one of these products to notice a difference in your OA symptoms. Another possible downside to SAM-e: This supplement can be expensive ($60 or more a month).

✔**MSM.** Found in tiny amounts in the blood and in most foods, methylsulfonylmethane (MSM) is believed to deliver sulfur to joints and act as an anti-inflammatory and pain reliever. Many patients say that taking this sulfur compound has helped their OA, but so far, few rigorously controlled studies have been done on it.

HOW TO TAKE ▶ The recommended dose for OA is 500 mg of MSM two or three times each day. You can also find MSM creams and gels that may be rubbed into affected areas, but it's not clear how effective these products are.

POSSIBLE CONCERNS ▶ MSM may have a blood-thinning effect and you may want to avoid it if you also take anticoagulant medications or supplements like Coumadin, aspirin, ginkgo, ginger, or vitamin E.

What About...

Apple cider vinegar. This folk remedy was popularized decades ago by a Vermont country doctor who claimed that a daily dose of apple cider vinegar (which is available as a liquid or in capsules) could ease arthritis symptoms, protect against osteoporosis, aid digestion, promote weight loss, and more. Unfortunately, there doesn't appear to be any clinical evidence that this substance has any therapeutic properties for OA or other health conditions.

Avocado/soybean unsaponifiables (ASU). This mixture of oils from avocado and soybeans has been shown in some studies to relieve pain and improve disability associated with OA, possibly by helping to stimulate cartilage repair. The supplement, which is sold as capsules without a prescription in Europe under the name Piascledine 300, isn't currently available in the United States, but it may be soon.

Bromelain. This pineapple enzyme—sold as a dietary supplement in tablet or capsule form—appears to have anti-inflammatory properties, and can be an effective treatment for bruises that won't heal and sprains with a lot of tissue swelling. But there's little evidence that bromelain relieves symptoms of OA.

Cherry extract. Both the sweet and tart varieties of cherries are rich in flavonoid compounds called anthocyanins and proanthocyanins, which act as antioxidants and natural anti-inflammatories. A well-publicized 1999 study suggests that eating 20 tart cherries might provide similar pain relief to taking an aspirin or ibuprofen by inhibiting inflammation-causing compounds in the body. The best-known therapeutic use for cherries is to prevent attacks of gout, and while more research needs to be done, it's thought that cherries might also help relieve rheumatoid arthritis (RA) and other conditions that involve inflammation. Liquid cherry extract may be less helpful for OA, which, unlike RA, isn't primarily an inflammatory condition. If you do choose to try cherry extract, you'll need to take 1,000 mg twice a day, about what you'd find in 4 cups of cherry juice or a pound of cherries.

Emu oil. This oil comes from the fat of emus, large, ostrich-like birds native to Australia. Sold in creams, capsules, and liquid form, emu oil is said to contain substances that help relieve arthritis pain, lower cholesterol, and speed wound healing. But despite glowing testimonials, there just isn't convincing scientific evidence in humans to support any of these health claims.

Evening primrose oil. It's true that evening primrose oil, black currant oil, and other sources of gamma-linolenic acid (GLA) are natural anti-inflammatories. Although they can be helpful for rheumatoid arthritis, they may be less effective for OA, which doesn't always have a prominent inflammatory component. If you want to try this treatment, take 500 mg of either evening primrose or black currant oil capsules twice a day.

Gelatin. Also known as hydrolyzed collagen, gelatin is a fibrous protein extracted from animal hooves, skin, and bones. It may contain some chondroitin (see page 51), but not at therapeutic levels, and there's little good research showing any benefit to OA from food-grade gelatin. Even though one gelatin product, called NutraJoint, has been shown to be somewhat helpful for osteoarthritis, its value may come from other ingredients in this product (such as vitamins C and D) that are cheaper when obtained from other sources.

DR. WEIL SAYS: "If you want to experiment with anti-inflammatory herbs for osteoarthritis, I recommend taking ginger or turmeric, or you can supplement with New Chapter's Zyflamend, which contains these and other anti-inflammatory herbs."

CHAPTER SEVEN

Considering Joint Surgery and Other Treatments

Despite your best efforts at controlling your OA symptoms, you may eventually come to a point where a surgical intervention seems like the best option. You may be reluctant and even scared to go under the knife, so how will you know when surgery is the appropriate next step? You and your physician should discuss the severity of your pain, any limitations on your mobility, and the treatments you've tried, both conventional and alternative.

In general, surgery is considered a last resort for people with OA and is usually recommended only when the medication (or supplements) you take are no longer effective; when you're unable to perform common functions like getting up from a chair or have difficulty taking the stairs; when pain keeps you awake at night; or when OA keeps you from seeing friends, taking vacations, working, or enjoying other aspects of your life. In these instances, surgery may have dramatic results, including often-permanent pain relief, increased movement of arthritic joints, and slowed progression of OA.

Of course, you'll need to weigh the benefits of surgery with the potential risks. While surgery can relieve OA pain and improve your movement, it's not right for everyone. Surgery can be too much of a strain for people who have other health problems, like heart or lung disease, severe osteoporosis, uncontrolled high blood pressure, or cancer, or who are older than age 95. It's also recommended that severely obese people (over 300 pounds) lose weight before any operation, since extra pounds stress the heart and lungs and can slow recovery. Your doctor can best discuss with you the individual risks and benefits associated with different types of joint surgery.

> "As to diseases, make a habit of two things—to help, or at least, to do no harm."
>
> HIPPOCRATES

Common Types of Joint Surgery

The following surgical procedures are three of the most common ones for people with OA. All three occur while you're under general, spinal, or local anesthesia and are usually done by an orthopedic surgeon.

Arthroscopy. This minimally invasive procedure can both examine and repair joint damage in one operation. Arthroscopy is most often performed on arthritic knees and shoulders to remove loose fragments of bone or cartilage, torn ligaments, inflamed tissue, or other debris that may be causing you pain and inflammation.

    WHAT WILL HAPPEN? ▸ Your surgeon will make a small incision on the side of your affected joint and insert a tube-shaped instrument called an arthroscope, which contains a tiny camera that relays images of the joint onto a television monitor. The surgeon can then see inside your joint and use surgical tools to repair any damaged bone, cartilage, or other material. Arthroscopy usually only takes an hour, you may receive a few stitches, and you'll be able to go home the same day, although you may need to use crutches for a week or so. The procedure can cause joint soreness and stiffness for a few days after surgery and carries a slight risk of infection and nerve injury.

    EXPECTATIONS ▸ Arthroscopy can treat some of the effects of OA, but it can't eliminate the root cause of joint problems. While some studies show that about half of people who undergo arthroscopy experience some pain relief, newer research suggests that arthroscopy isn't any more effective at reducing pain or increasing functioning than "sham" (pretend) surgery. This has led some experts to conclude that arthroscopic surgery works by a placebo mechanism, healing that occurs simply because you believe in a treatment.

Osteotomy. In people with knee OA, cartilage tends to break down more in the inner portion of the knee joint, which can result in a bow-legged appearance. An osteotomy surgically repositions the bones within the knee joint, allowing your weight to spread more evenly across the knee. It's best performed on people with knee OA who are younger than age 60 and physically active.

    WHAT WILL HAPPEN? ▸ Surgeons will remove a wedge of bone from the outer portion of your damaged knee joint, bring the remaining bones together, and secure them with pins or staples. The procedure takes about an hour and a half, and you'll likely spend about three days in the hospital. After surgery, you'll need to wear a cast or splint on your knee and use crutches for one to three months. You can put your full weight on the joint about 12 weeks after surgery, although it may take up to a year for your knee to fully adjust to its new position. There's a small risk of nerve damage, infection, and blood clots following surgery, as well as a possibility that the knee may not look completely symmetrical afterward.

EXPECTATIONS ▶ An osteotomy can relieve knee pain and help slow the progression of OA, but its main goal is to delay the need for a total knee replacement in younger people.

Total joint replacement. This surgery can ease pain and increase mobility in people with OA who find that exercise, medications, and lifestyle measures are no longer helpful. It's most popular for arthritic knees and hips, but can also be used to replace shoulders, elbows, and knuckles.

WHAT WILL HAPPEN? ▶ Surgeons remove diseased portions of your cartilage and bone and replace them with a new, artificial joint made from metal, plastic, or ceramic material. The operation takes about two hours and you'll likely spend about three or four days in the hospital. As with most operations, there's a small risk of infection and blood clots after surgery. Over the next several months, the remaining bone will naturally grow around the artificial joint, integrating it into your body.

EXPECTATIONS ▶ Some 90 percent of people who undergo total knee or hip replacement experience less pain and a significant improvement in their ability to perform common activities. But total joint replacement won't restore the full range of motion you had before you developed OA, and you'll need to permanently avoid high-impact aerobics, running, and other sports that stress the joints (walking, swimming, and golf are fine). In addition, you might occasionally hear the "click" of the metal and plastic parts when you move, and any metal in your artificial joint may activate metal detectors.

Try This: Hospital Room Makeover

Get a room with a view.
If you'll be spending a few days in the hospital, arrange for a room with a view of grass, trees, or water rather than the parking lot, if possible.

Turn down the volume.
If hospital noises make it difficult to sleep, consider bringing along a white-noise machine.

Add some fragrance.
You can counter sterile hospital smells by putting a drop or two of fragrant oils such as lavender or vanilla on your bedding.

Bring something from home.
You might bring along your favorite pajamas or quilt, put art, flowers, or photos of loved ones around, and bring in headphones and your favorite music, books, or videotapes (including comedies).

Jump-start your appetite.
If you find that your hospital's meals are less than appetizing and there aren't any restrictions on your diet, have friends and family bring in healthy, appealing food.

DR. WEIL SAYS: "I consider surgery a method of last resort when OA is severely painful and disabling. Surgical hip replacement can be highly effective when the joint is destroyed, while knee replacement is slightly less effective. Surgical risk and recovery times may be more difficult the older you are."

Staying Healthy Before and After Surgery

Once you and your physician have decided that surgery is right for you, you'll want to prepare as thoroughly as you can for the experience, especially if you're undergoing a major operation like a total knee or hip replacement. Fortunately, there are many ways you can take control during the days and weeks preceding surgery, and even during the operation itself. In fact, a growing body of research indicates that patients who take an active role in preparing for surgery experience faster healing, reduced postoperative pain, less need for medication, and shorter hospital stays.

Try to schedule your surgery during a time of relatively good health, to give your immune system a head start toward recovery. In addition, here are some of the most effective ways to ease preoperative jitters and help you heal, enlisting as resources everything from friends to the power of the mind.

Choose a patient advocate. Ask a friend or family member, or a patient advocate supplied by the hospital, to act on your behalf with doctors, nurses, and other staff members. Your advocate should become familiar with the hospital's handbook of patient services and make sure you get any available care you require. Plus, your advocate can see to it that your wishes and needs are considered and that your questions are answered.

Build a support network. Social and emotional support is key, as hospitals can be dehumanizing and stressful environments. Studies find that hospitalized patients who get enough emotional support heal faster, need fewer surgeries, and experience less pain. When people ask how they can help, don't hesitate to assign specific tasks. You'll also want to have someone with you in the hospital just before surgery and when you come out, and schedule someone to be on hand for as many days as needed during your recovery.

Ask questions. It's a good idea to keep a notepad on your bed tray to jot down questions for your medical team as they arise; sometimes it's hard to organize your thoughts when doctors drop in early in the morning or late at night. Also, you can protect yourself from medical mistakes by asking staff in a friendly manner about various aspects of your treatment—What's in the intravenous fluid bag? What's the purpose of this procedure, test, or medication? What do my test results show? Are you aware of my drug allergies?

Supplement wisely. You may need to taper or stop the use of other herbal supplements (blood thinners like ginkgo or herbs such as St. John's wort that interfere with the metabolism of certain medications). However, tonics such as ginseng and cordyceps mushroom may help you recuperate faster. These supplements are safe, but you should tell your doctor if you're taking them. You can begin taking a tonic on the day you enter the hospital, and use it as directed on the package. Plus, you may recover from surgery faster if you get additional vitamin C—given intravenously with your doctor's approval, or taken orally at a dose of 1,000 mg twice a day.

Stay on top of pain. Don't be afraid to ask for the pain medication you need. In addition, guided-imagery tapes have been found in some studies to reduce pain, improve immune function, and speed healing. People who use these recordings spend fewer days in the hospital, one reason why some health insurers now make free tapes available to plan members preparing for surgery. Plus, stress-reduction techniques such as breath work and meditation may also help reduce pain and promote healing as you recover.

Make sure infection-control measures are followed. It's perfectly okay to say something like, "Doctor, I'm probably being paranoid, but it would make me feel better if you would wash your hands (or put on fresh gloves) before examining me."

Make a tape of healing statements. A growing number of medical professionals believe that patients under anesthesia are able to hear and are in a highly suggestible state. And studies support this idea, including one at Beth Israel Medical Center in New York showing that patients who heard positive affirmations on a tape played while they were under anesthesia required 50 percent less postoperative medication than a control group. Listening to relaxing music before and after a surgical procedure can also reduce pain.

Receive healing energy. Energy medicine therapies such as Therapeutic Touch (see page 49) and Reiki are powerful ways to promote relaxation and enhance the healing process. In fact, a number of studies have documented Therapeutic Touch's ability to boost immunity, relieve pain, and speed healing of surgical wounds. You might consider trying at least one session of these noninvasive therapies. If you can, schedule a daily treatment for the two or three days before and after your operation. Some hospitals now offer these services, or you may have to locate an independent practitioner.

Intra-Articular Treatments

Before you decide on surgery, you may want to consider one other type of conventional pain treatment for OA. Intra-articular treatments—meaning "within the joint"—involve a physician injecting pain- and inflammation-relieving substances directly into an arthritic joint. There are two types of intra-articular treatments: One is corticosteroid injections, and the other is viscosupplementation. Both treatments will provide temporary relief that lasts anywhere from a few weeks to a few months.

Corticosteroid shots. These injections of steroid hormones can be very effective at reducing significant swelling and pain, but are less helpful for other symptoms and may worsen OA in the long run. The effects of these shots are temporary, and because long-term corticosteroid use can actually increase joint damage and infection, you shouldn't have more than four injections in each joint per year. Nevertheless, steroid injections are unlikely to cause the side effects associated with oral steroids because they are taken less frequently.

Viscosupplementation. Hyaluronic acid, a substance found in healthy joint fluid, is injected into an affected joint to help thicken the joint fluid and lubricate the joint. You'll need one shot a week for three to five weeks, with repeat courses possible after six months. Viscosupplementation holds promise for easing the pain of OA without the risks of steroids. It appears most helpful for people with mild to moderate OA, and can sometimes cause minor pain and swelling at the injection site.

At Home: The Road to Recovery

You won't be dancing a jig immediately following joint surgery, but you'll be far more active than you might think. In fact, exercise is *recommended* for those who have had total joint replacement or other operations, since it helps your body heal, helps your muscles regain their strength and mobility, and prevents potentially deadly blood clots in the legs when you've been bedridden.

As soon as the day after surgery, your doctor should arrange for you to meet with a physical therapist in the hospital, who will teach you exercises that you can do in bed and help you learn how to use crutches or a cane as you continue to heal. You should keep up such activity once you go home, resting when necessary, but avoiding staying in bed all day. Instead, try to move around frequently on crutches, in your home and later outside. If you've had an arthroscopy, you should be able to resume regular physical activity, like walking, cycling, or swimming, within a month. Recovering from an osteotomy or total joint replacement can take longer, but expect to be fully exercising again within two months of surgery.

You'll want to keep your surgical wound clean and dry—you may need to avoid taking a shower or bath for several weeks until stitches are removed; take sponge baths instead. Plus, you can reduce pain and swelling by keeping your leg on a footrest or pillow (if surgery was on your knee or hip) and by applying ice as needed. Watch for signs of infection, like running a fever, or redness or draining of the wound, and of a blood clot, such as calf or chest pain or shortness of breath. By following these tips, you'll keep your joint healthy and speed healing, so you'll be back on your feet—dancing that jig—even sooner.

Try This: Home, Safe Home

Before you leave the hospital or even before you go there to have surgery, ask a friend or loved one to help prepare your home for your return. This means placing frequently used objects at arm level to keep you from reaching too far up or down; installing a shower chair, grip bars, and raised toilet seat in the bathroom; removing throw rugs and securing electrical cords to prevent falls; and rearranging furniture to make it easy to maneuver around in crutches.

To set up a "recovery station" by your bed or favorite chair, place a telephone, radio, television remote control, reading materials, tissues, water pitcher and glass, and medications, so that they're all within close reach. You might also consider investing in some assistive devices to help you reach without bending, like a grabbing tool, long-handled sponge, or long-handled shoehorn (see page 67 for more).

Living with Osteoarthritis

Having OA can change your life in many different ways—from the way you move, to the activities you do, to the pain you face on a regular basis. Tasks that once gave you joy, like gardening, may now hurt arthritic knees, and even daily chores like housework can be difficult when your hands are swollen and painful. OA can also affect other areas of your life. You may find relationships that were once simple are now more complex: Will your family and friends understand that OA pain may limit your ability to enjoy certain activities? How will this pain affect your sex life? Will having OA interfere with your work in any way? In this chapter, you'll find answers to those questions as well as other advice for various aspects of living with OA.

> "Keep making the movements of life."
>
> HENRY JAMES

OA and Your Family

Living with OA can be challenging for you, but it can also be hard for your loved ones. Your family and friends may find it upsetting to see you in pain, feel helpless when they can't make things better, and even experience anger or resentment at the effect your OA has had on your relationship with them. Actually, these emotions are all perfectly normal, and they don't have to weaken a friendship or marriage. Instead, improving communication, sharing tasks, and learning new ways of doing things can not only help you cope more easily with OA, they can strengthen your current relationships and even foster new ones. Consider the following advice:

Educate others. You'll want to explain to your loved ones that OA is a chronic condition that may get better when you follow a healthy lifestyle and

OSTEOARTHRITIS: AN INTEGRATIVE MEDICINE TREATMENT PROGRAM **63** take pain-relieving drugs, but won't go away completely. In fact, show your friends and family this book and other resources, so they understand what's going on in your body and why you may feel worse some times than others. If they know what to expect from your condition, they'll likely be more accepting when you feel cranky from morning stiffness or have to turn down an invitation because you're not feeling up to it.

Communication is key. Whether a sore hip has prevented you from mowing the lawn the way you used to or achy knees have kept you from joining your spouse at your Friday dancing lesson, it's normal for your loved ones to feel some resentment. True, they don't like to see you in pain, but they're probably also frustrated and disappointed that you may not be able to keep up with your usual routine. This can be particularly stressful if you're the main breadwinner in your family and OA pain has caused you to cut back on work or leave your job altogether. Rather than pretending that everything's fine, it's best to talk regularly and openly about OA with your loved ones. It's a good idea to discuss the possible implications of your condition *before* problems occur, so you and your family will be prepared for such changes early on. By keeping communication lines open, you'll address your needs—and those of your loved ones—in a positive way, before they spiral into bigger problems.

Accept new realities. It can be difficult, but you'll need to accept that OA may bring new challenges and limitations into your life. That doesn't mean giving up a healthy lifestyle or hoping for a cure. Instead, you may learn to accept that you'll need to do things differently than in the past. Specifically, be honest about what you can and can't do. If you used to clean the house by yourself every week, figure out what tasks you may still be able to do and what chores you'll need a hand with. Enlist family members to take on household responsibilities that may be too painful for you. If stiff, achy knees or hands are interfering with your Saturday afternoon bowling league, you may need to reconsider your participation. Accept the loss, mourn for it, and brainstorm new ways to enjoy socializing with your friends. Perhaps you'll become a scorekeeper rather than an active participant, or meet the team afterward for dinner instead.

Live a healthy lifestyle together. It's a lot easier to develop new healthy habits and reinforce current ones when you have others supporting you. If you're just starting

Try This: Hot Pepper Rub

Hot peppers may taste great in salsa, but they're also potent pain relievers. Capsaicin, the ingredient that gives chili peppers their fiery taste, appears to deplete a compound in the body called "substance P" that transmits pain signals to the brain. You can take advantage of the healing power of peppers by using over-the-counter creams or gels containing capsaicin on arthritic joints, especially those located close to the skin surface, such as the knee. Apply the cream lightly to joints no less than three times a day. The cream may initially cause a burning sensation, but this will subside the more you use it. Be sure to wash your hands well after use, and avoid contact with eyes or any areas of broken or irritated skin. Look for products containing 0.025 percent capsaicin at drugstores and supermarkets (one popular brand is Zostrix).

an exercise program for OA, ask a friend or family member to accompany you on a daily walk or bike ride. Want to eat healthier and lose weight? Bring your spouse along to the grocery store, flip through cookbooks together, or make meal preparation a family affair. Not only will you stick to your new lifestyle, you'll have a positive effect on your loved ones' health, too.

Get support. A great way to learn new ways of doing things is to seek out others who have successfully done the same. Consider joining a local OA support group (see page 37), or simply connecting with other people who have the condition. You'll make new friends, learn tips for coping, and you'll also see how other families have adjusted to a similar situation.

Accentuate the positive. OA can't get you down if you don't let it. Try to rally with family and friends; together you can tackle the ups and downs of living with this condition. Some people find that a sense of humor can ease even the most difficult aspects of living with pain, while others gain inspiration through spirituality or religious faith.

Recognize the power of touch. Sex is a sensitive subject for many people with OA. Granted, the frustration and depression that can accompany OA can make you feel less interested—and possibly physically unable to engage—in sex. But it's important not to give up on intimacy. Remember that you don't have to abandon a fulfilling and loving sex life; you just may need to make some adjustments. You'll want to sit down with your partner and explain your worries and concerns about the new challenges that sex may pose for you. Specifically, tell him or her what feels good for you and what causes you discomfort. Explore other ways of being intimate, like massaging each other, cuddling, or simply holding hands and talking. And when you do try intercourse, plan to take your pain medications so they reach their peak effect during sex (about halfway through the dose).

OA at the Office

It's hard enough to express the pain and frustration you feel from OA to your loved ones. But dealing with your boss and coworkers can be an even stickier subject. Will OA affect your responsibilities at work? Can you be fired if you take too much time off or if your aching joints prevent you from performing at your usual level?

Actually, most experts advise that you *don't* need to tell your boss or coworkers about your OA if it isn't obvious (i.e., you don't walk with a cane or have noticeable physical changes), doesn't interfere with your ability to do

Rain and Pain

Does your knee feel stiffer, your hands achier, or your neck sorer when the sun is nowhere in sight? Many people with OA and other chronic pain conditions find their symptoms are worse on days when the weather is cold, damp, or rainy. Indeed, some research shows that more than 80 percent of people with OA experience an increase in symptoms due to weather, suggesting that temperature, rain, and barometric pressure may affect pain. But other studies have found no such link. Theoretically, changes in barometric pressure could affect joint fluid and inflammation, but we just don't know for sure. If you find that certain weather seems to worsen your OA, you may want to be extra-vigilant with self-care measures on those days.

your job, and as long as you don't need special accommodations or assistance at work. But if it seems that your coworkers feel you're not carrying your weight or are getting special treatment, it's probably a good idea to discuss your OA with your supervisor to head off any complaints.

Start by scheduling a meeting with your boss to describe your condition briefly, including ways in which you think it may affect your work, whether that means you're less able to lift heavy items or will require extra time off for surgery. Make it clear that you're not looking for sympathy but are trying to do your best for the company and yourself. Then provide your boss with some simple solutions you've come up with to help you do your job better. These may include assistive devices like easy-to-grip pens and ergonomic keyboards and chairs, and exercises you practice at home to make movement easier at work. Your supervisor should be willing to allow for such changes—in fact, he may be required by law to do so. (For more on how the Americans with Disabilities Act protects the rights of workers with arthritis, call the ADA information line at *800-514-0301*.)

Making Daily Living Easier

Yes, OA can make it difficult to do even ordinary tasks, but that doesn't mean you have to stop being independent. Although it's always nice to have a friend or family member willing to lend a hand, the truth is that you can still take part in many daily activities once you learn how to protect your joints and move them in new ways.

First, you'll need to pace yourself. Moving nonstop from dawn till dusk isn't good for your body or your mind. Try to balance periods of activity with rest so that you don't get too tired or stressed and your joints don't become too painful. And pay attention to your body while you work. Do a quick scan: How do your joints and muscles feel? Do you notice any areas of tension or pain? If you do, it's time for a break.

For times when you need a little help, like opening jars, grasping a pen, and making other movements that might be painful, consider investing in some assistive devices, handy gadgets and tools that can make difficult

Try This: Hot & Cold Therapy

Hot and Cold Packs. Some people use cold packs to temporarily ease arthritis pain and stiffness; others find heat more helpful. Applying cold to achy joints numbs the area and reduces pain, while applying heat relaxes muscles, relieves aches, and stimulates blood circulation, which can help irritated tissues heal. Which you use is a matter of personal preference. If you like cold, try a cold pack from the drugstore, or even a bag of frozen peas. For heat, try a soak in a whirlpool or warm bath, or apply a microwaveable hot pack or adhesive patch like Thermacare. For safety's sake, apply hot or frozen compresses for no longer than 20 minutes, and keep a thin towel between the compress and your skin.

Paraffin Bath. Paraffin wax isn't just for manicures. It also retains heat well, making it a useful topical remedy for joint stiffness and pain. Slowly melt the wax in a small paraffin-bath tub (available at department, medical-supply, and beauty-supply stores) on low heat. Wait till the wax has cooled a bit, then dip your hand, elbow, foot, or other achy part into the wax. You can also use a paintbrush to apply the wax to larger joints. Repeat up to a dozen times, then wrap the arthritic joint in plastic wrap, cover it with a towel, and let it cool. The paraffin will lock in heat, bringing temporary relief to painful areas.

movements easier. You'll want to use tools that have long handles (which prevent you from having to bend) or wide, easier-to-grip handles (so you don't have to grip them as tightly). An occupational therapist can also teach you techniques to maintain daily living and work skills (ask your doctor for a referral). To get you started, refer to the tips in the box below.

Tips to Help with Everyday Activities

Here are some tips for making everyday activities easier.

BATHING

- Sit on a bath stool in your shower or tub to relieve pressure on your knees and hips.

- Install grab bars near your tub and toilet to help you stand up more easily.

- Use an elevated toilet seat to ease stress on your knee joints.

- Try an electric toothbrush to cut down on gripping and back-and-forth hand motions.

- Place skid-proof bath mats in your tub and shower to prevent falls.

DRESSING

- Consider using elastic shoelaces, which are easier to grip than cloth ones. Velcro-closure shoes are another good idea.

- Try using a long-handled shoehorn so you don't have to bend to put shoes on.

- Use a buttonhook tool to avoid having to grasp buttons with your hands.

- Attach large, circular zipper pulls to your zippers. Larger pulls are easier to grasp.

COOKING

- Use easy-to-grip kitchen tools and utensils with large, comfortable handles.

- Sit on a high stool when cooking or washing dishes to reduce stress on your knees and hips.

- Invest in an under-the-counter jar opener that works by gripping the lid as you turn the jar.

- Buy some prepared foods to reduce prep time, like pre-washed, pre-shredded salad greens or other veggies.

- Choose lightweight pots, pans, and mixing bowls.

CLEANING HOUSE

- Don't clean your whole house at once.

- Use long-handled tools like feather dusters, mops, and brooms rather than scrubbing on your hands and knees or grasping a dust cloth.

- Keep several sets of cleaning supplies throughout your house so you don't have to move them to each room you clean.

DRIVING

- Invest in an easy-to-grip car door opener and starter, a long-handled tool that holds your key and makes it easier to grip.

- Lean on a lumbar pillow to relieve lower-back strain.

- On long trips, get out of the car and stretch every hour.

GARDENING

- Use long-handled, easy-grip garden tools to minimize stress on your joints.

- Keep your tools in a wheelbarrow or bucket to help you move them in one trip.

- Keep a chair handy—you can lean on it when getting up from the ground.

- Weed after you water the garden; moist soil makes it easier to pull out weeds.

Posture Pointers: Standing Tall

Good posture can make all the difference in how easily you move and how much pain you feel. People with OA don't always have the best posture, because they may favor—and put more weight on—an unaffected knee or hip rather than an arthritic one. Yet, good posture is crucial to minimizing strain on your joints and spine and reducing muscle pain and injury. Besides, putting more pressure on one leg than another may stress its joints so much that your *healthy* leg may eventually develop OA, too. Instead, try these suggestions, which can help anyone improve or maintain good posture.

Get fit. Good posture calls for strong and flexible muscles, joints, and ligaments, which work together to support and lengthen your spine, keep it centered, and allow you to move efficiently. In contrast, slouching can shorten chest muscles and reduce flexibility. Regular activity and exercise programs such as yoga and Pilates can strengthen and stretch muscles plus enhance posture. Also, movement re-education programs such as the Alexander Technique (see page 46) may help improve the way you sit, stand, and walk.

Stand tall. When standing, good posture means holding your head and neck straight, relaxing your shoulder blades, keeping your knees straight (not locked), tucking in your stomach and rear, and distributing weight evenly over your feet. Once you get used to standing this way, you'll notice that your joints are less painful. If you're lifting objects, keep your legs apart, back straight, and stomach muscles tight, and be sure to bend at your knees, not your waist.

Sit properly. When you're sitting, avoid slouching by holding your head up, knees comfortably apart, feet on the floor (or a footrest), and pelvis tilted slightly forward. Keep your hips, knees, and ankles, as well as your elbows, at a 90-degree angle to your torso. It's also okay to use a small pillow or rolled-up towel on your chair to help support your lower back. And if pain in your knees or hips makes it difficult to stand up, try using a higher chair.

Rest easy. It's generally best to sleep on your side with knees bent, since sleeping on your stomach curves your back unnaturally. You can also use a rolled-up towel or neck pillow to cushion your neck and spine, and make sure that your mattress is firm enough to comfortably support your spine.

CHAPTER NINE

Exploring New Research Horizons

As you complete this book, you might be wondering if scientists will find a cure—or even better treatments—for OA. What if instead of taking pain medications, you could visit your doctor, who would inject healthy new cartilage into your joints? Or maybe, instead of waiting until you've developed a sore hip, you could take a blood test to identify OA and get started on a program to head off joint damage before it begins.

This may not be wishful thinking: These options may be available in your lifetime. That's great news, because there have been few breakthroughs in the study of OA since it was first identified in 1886. In fact, the top recommendation for OA 100 years ago is still one of today's first treatments: aspirin.

But things are changing, with new theories about the causes of OA and slow-but-steady progress in medical research. Within the past two decades, scientists have reconsidered the way they view the arthritic process. Once believed to be the result of simple "wear-and-tear" to aging joints, OA is now seen as a complex disease with multiple causes. And new treatment approaches are slowly becoming available: In addition to the advent of COX-2 inhibitors like Celebrex, scientists have also developed pain-relieving methods such as injections of hyaluronic acid. They've also improved surgical procedures by reducing recovery time for operations and improving the artificial parts used to replace worn-out joints.

There's still a long way to go, but experts have faith that scientific advances will eventually help change the way OA is prevented and treated. For the latest state of the science, *Self Healing* spoke with John Klippel, MD, president and CEO of the Arthritis Foundation. While he doesn't think that a cure for OA is just around the corner, Dr. Klippel says that researchers are hard at work

> "In three words I can sum up everything I've learned about life: it goes on."
>
> ROBERT FROST

trying to identify its exact causes, which in turn may help scientists develop new drugs and even supplements to treat and slow joint damage, rather than simply treat pain and other symptoms. Also, Dr. Klippel agrees that lifestyle measures as well as supplements like glucosamine and chondroitin are important parts of any integrative treatment plan for OA. Here are five promising areas of research that you may hear more about over the next few years.

Learning what causes OA. Right now, researchers know that aging cartilage and bones, excess weight on the joints, and previous injuries to them can increase your risk of developing OA. But it's still unclear what predisposes some people to get the condition instead of others. In fact, it's not even certain there's one single cause. Dr. Klippel cites still-unidentified genes (OA runs in families), hormonal effects (more women than men have OA), and even a yet-unknown systemic (whole-body) process as possible contributing factors, all of which could determine how easily cartilage, bone, and other parts of your joints are damaged. Scientists are likely many years away from pinpointing the causes of OA, but when they do, it will open up new avenues for treatment.

Screening those at risk. Once researchers understand the biological process that leads to OA, it will be easier to identify who is likely to get the disease and who isn't. That means they could greatly improve screening tests like MRI scans—already in the works—to better show doctors the extent of a patient's joint damage, even before symptoms appear. People with a family history of OA could be screened in their 30s or 40s, to start on an lifestyle program to prevent arthritis decades before trouble begins. Also, scientists are trying to identify the genes responsible for OA, so that physicians could test people for the relevant genes and get them started with lifestyle changes sooner.

Even better, identifying people with OA could be as simple as taking a routine blood test. Researchers recently discovered that biological markers ("biomarkers"), substances that signal cartilage damage and repair, are present in the blood and urine of people with OA. They've found that people with OA have lower blood and urine levels of a substance that helps with cartilage production and higher levels of a substance that causes cartilage damage than people without joint disease. That's important, since it means that scientists could identify people with OA earlier, distinguish mild forms of OA from severe, and assess whether a particular treatment is working or not. Dr. Klippel says that these biomarkers could also help researchers determine why some people with OA never have symptoms, while others suffer severe joint damage. It may be that people with OA who don't have symptoms have a natural joint-repair process that others lack. Ideally, studying such people could help scientists create new ways to treat and repair joint damage from OA.

Developing new drugs. You already know about some drugs that treat OA, like NSAIDs and COX-2 inhibitors. While these medications help soothe painful joints, they can't truly get to the root of the problem. Researchers hope that once they've better identified the causes of OA, they'll be able to create new drugs that will actually help slow or reverse joint damage as well.

Slowing OA's progression. Researchers are very interested in chondroprotective agents, approaches that can protect cartilage from further breakdown and could help slow or prevent joint damage. But that doesn't mean these agents will only be available in drug form: As Dr. Klippel points out, many of the lifestyle measures in this book, such as exercise, are thought to protect cartilage, as are the supplements glucosamine and chondroitin. In fact, the first large US clinical trial to look at the effects of glucosamine and chondroitin is now under way. Known as GAIT (Glucosamine/Chondroitin Arthritis Intervention Trial), this two-year study will look at the effects of these supplements in combination and alone and will also determine whether they can actually reduce or slow progression of knee OA. You can expect to read about GAIT's results in the next several years.

Growing new cartilage. It be great if scientists could create healthy new replacements for your worn cartilage. Truth is, researchers are trying to make cartilage replacement a reality. Over the next decade, you'll hear more about this technique, which could involve growing healthy cartilage cells in the lab and then injecting them into joints to repair damage. Eventually, cartilage replacement could be a nonsurgical option for some people with OA.

These new areas of research are exciting, but it may take years before their results can be applied. Indeed, the slow speed of research can be frustrating, but rigorous studies are an important part of the scientific process. With every discovery—in the lab, in animal studies, and in clinical trials—researchers are getting closer to finding better remedies and possibly a cure for OA.

What can you do in the meantime? Follow the lifestyle measures, supplement recommendations, and conventional treatment advice in this book, which can greatly relieve pain, stiffness, and other OA symptoms. Talk with others who have OA to learn new tips for coping with the condition. Investigate the resources on page 74 for more support. And stay on top of the research news through organizations like the Arthritis Foundation (see page 74), and then discuss this information with your doctor. Remember, there's much you can do to help yourself live more comfortably with osteoarthritis.

OA Treatment Summary

To help you start on your way to feeling better, here's an at-a-glance compilation of Dr. Weil's best advice for easing and treating osteoarthritis.

KEY

★ Dr. Weil's top recommendations

✔ Other approaches that are safe and worth trying

Self-Care

★ Never underestimate the innate ability of your body to help heal itself

★ Be honest and communicative about your abilities and limitations

★ Keep a diary to monitor your symptoms—like pain, joint stiffness, swelling, and fatigue—and track what triggers them

✔ Maintain a positive mental view of your health by cultivating a sense of humor or seeking solace through spirituality or religious faith

✔ Learn the keys to proper posture

✔ Use heat, cold, hot pepper rubs, acupressure, and other self-care measures to alleviate pain and stiffness

✔ Experiment with special assistive devices, for eating or grooming, if needed (see page 76)

Conventional Treatment

★ Attend physical therapy as needed

✔ Take acetaminophen or non-steroidal anti-inflammatory drugs (aspirin, ibuprofen) as needed

✔ View surgery only as a last resort for severe pain and disability, and weigh its benefits and risks

Diet

★ Achieve and maintain a healthy weight:

- Identify proper portions of food and drink, and make a conscious effort to reduce your portion sizes

- Keep a food diary for a few weeks or more by recording every food and beverage you consume, the portion size, when you consumed it, and how hungry you were at the time

- Learn to eat mindfully and slowly by focusing on your meal with no outside distractions like TV or reading material

- Be physically active for 30 minutes, at least three times a week (see physical activity)

★ Eat an anti-inflammatory diet:

- Choose more monounsaturated fats (in olive oil and some nuts)

- Choose more omega-3 fatty acids (in flax, walnuts, and oily, cold-water fish like salmon and sardines)

- Eat more fruits, vegetables, whole grains, legumes, and soy foods

- Avoid trans fats, or partially hydrogenated oils (found in margarines, potato chips, cookies, crackers, and many other processed foods)

- Limit polyunsaturated vegetable oils (safflower, sunflower, and corn oils) and products made from them

- Eat less meat and fewer full-fat dairy products and processed foods

- Use anti-inflammatory spices like ginger and turmeric to season meals

- Drink plenty of water every day (at least 8 glasses) to stay well hydrated and help keep joints lubricated

✔ Take a daily vitamin and mineral regimen as insurance, including 200 mg of vitamin C, 400 to 800 IU of natural vitamin E (or 80 mg of tocopherols and tocotrienols), 25,000 IU of mixed carotenes, and 400 IU of vitamin D

Physical Activity
(in water or on land)

★ Get aerobic activity (walking, cycling, swimming, etc.) for 30 minutes at least three times a week

★ Strength train for 20 minutes two or three times a week

★ Practice flexibility and balance exercises, like yoga, tai chi, or stretching, on a daily basis

✔ Consider taking a special arthritis-oriented class like a warm water workout or participating in the Arthritis Foundation's PACE (People with Arthritis Can Exercise) program (see page 75)

Mind–Body Measures

★ Practice one or more mind-body relaxation techniques each day:

• If you're new to mind-body exercises, start with breath work or progressive muscle relaxation, which require no fancy equipment or classes, are easy to learn and inexpensive, and don't take much time to do

• If you're already familiar with mind-body techniques, are willing to spend more time practicing them, or would like to deepen your work by seeing a trained professional, try meditation, guided imagery, hypnosis, or biofeedback

✔ Consider joining a local or online support group for people with OA

✔ Recognize the possible signs and symptoms of depression, and seek help if necessary

Alternative Therapies

★ Choose one or more alternative therapies based on your individual symptoms and needs:

• For pain relief: acupuncture, chiropractic, massage, TENS, Therapeutic Touch

• For stiffness: chiropractic, massage

• To improve posture and movement: Alexander Technique, Feldenkrais Method

Supplements

Note: It is safe, but not necessary, to take all of these supplements together.

★ Glucosamine and chondroitin sulfates:

• If you weigh less than 120 pounds, take 1,000 mg a day of glucosamine and 800 mg of chondroitin in two or three divided doses;

• If you weigh more than 120 pounds, but less than 200, take 1,500 mg a day of glucosamine and 1,200 mg of chondroitin;

• If you weigh more than 200 pounds, take 2,000 mg a day of glucosamine and 1,600 mg of chondroitin

★ Zyflamend (contains ginger, turmeric, and other anti-inflammatory herbs): One softgel, twice a day with food

✔ SAM-e: Start by taking 400 mg twice a day for two weeks, then decrease to a maintenance dose of 200 mg twice a day thereafter

✔ MSM: Take 500 mg two or three times each day

Resource Guide

General Information

ORGANIZATIONS

Arthritis Foundation
PO Box 7669
Atlanta, Georgia 30357-0669
(800) 283-7800
www.arthritis.org
Leading national organization on arthritis offers up-to-date research and resources, product information, event listings, and referrals to your local chapter. Their website has message boards and other forms of online support. You can also order Arthritis Foundation publications.

American College of Rheumatology
1800 Century Place, Suite 250
Atlanta, Georgia 30345
(404) 633-3777
www.rheumatology.org
Offers current information on patient care and specific diseases and publishes several journals on arthritis and rheumatism; website locates board-certified rheumatologists.

National Institute of Arthritis and Musculoskeletal and Skin Diseases Information Clearinghouse
US Department of Health and Human Services' National Institutes of Health
1 AMS Circle
Bethesda, Maryland 20892-3675
(301) 495-4484 or
(877) 22-NIAMS (toll free)
www.niams.nih.gov
Provides up-to-date information about arthritis research, diet, exercise, coping with pain, and arthritis in children; plus the website offers some information in Spanish.

All About Arthritis.com
www.allaboutarthritis.com
Website offers advice about pain management, living with arthritis, medications, and has special information for caregivers.

BOOKS

The Arthritis Foundation's Guide to Good Living with Osteoarthritis
Includes an "ask the doctor" worksheet with questions to ask before surgery; a guide to the latest osteoarthritis drugs; information about which herbs and supplements really work; and effective strategies for pain relief.

The Arthritis Foundation's Guide to Managing Your Arthritis
Offers advice for managing many different types of arthritis, including OA. Has information on both medications and supplements, easy exercises to help you control pain and stiffness, and tips for successful arthritis surgery and recovery.

Guide to Pain Management (from the Arthritis Foundation)
Has information for people who cope with pain on a daily basis.

Managing Pain Before It Manages You, Revised Edition
Margaret A. Caudill, MD, PhD
(The Guilford Press, 2001)
A workbook-type program to help manage chronic pain and lead a fuller life.

Coping with Osteoarthritis: Revised and Updated
Robert Phillips, PhD
(Avery Books, 2001)
Provides information on osteoarthritis, medication, exercise, diet, and lifestyle changes.

The Columbia Presbyterian Osteoarthritis Handbook: The Complete Guide to the Most Common Form of Arthritis
Ronald P. Grelsamer, MD, and Suzanne Loebl, editors
(John Wiley and Sons, 1997)
Presents an overview of treatments (drug therapy, exercise, rest, pain relief, diet) for OA and explores the pros and cons of joint surgery.

Stop Osteoarthritis Now! Halting the Baby Boomer's Disease
Harris H. McIlwain, MD, and Debra Fulghum Bruce (Fireside, 1996)
Outlines a five-step treatment plan for self-care involving moist heat, exercise, weight control, medication, and joint protection.

Strong Women and Men Beat Arthritis
Miriam E. Nelson, PhD , et al.
(Berkley Publishing Group, 2003)
This comprehensive, hands-on guide describes how to prevent and treat arthritis.

Exercise and OA

ORGANIZATIONS

American Council on Exercise (ACE)
4851 Paramount Drive
San Diego, California 92123
(800) 825-3636 or (858) 535-8227
http://acefitness.org
Offers information about exercising with arthritis.

BOOKS

Exercise Beats Arthritis
Valerie Sayce and Ian Fraser
(Bull Publishing, 1998)
Contains an easy-to-follow program to help arthritis sufferers cope with this condition. Includes over 225 illustrations and a special section on water exercise.

Arthritis: An American Yoga Association Wellness Guide
Alice Christensen (Kensington Publishing Corp., 2001)
A program based on traditional yoga techniques to help people with arthritis feel and move better.

Overcoming Arthritis
Dr. Paul Lam and Judith Horstman
(DK Publishing, 2002)
Offers a clear overview of the various forms of arthritis and its treatments, both conventional and alternative, plus a practical step-by-step tai chi program for people with arthritis.

VIDEOS AND DVDS

PACE: People with Arthritis Can Exercise I (from the Arthritis Foundation)
Led by champion golfer Jan Stephenson, this video demonstrates basic, gentle routines that include stretching, strengthening, and exercises to help you regain your ability to do everyday activities.

PACE II
Learn the next level of PACE routines including an endurance-building segment for a more advanced workout.

Tai Chi for Arthritis
Tai chi instructor and physician Paul Lam leads 12 tai chi exercises for people with arthritis.

**Living Yoga —
Back Care Yoga for Beginners**
Famed yoga instructor Rodney Yee teaches a gentle yoga program designed for people with back pain.

OTHER

"Make Waves: A Warm Water Workout" (from the Arthritis Foundation)
This laminated, waterproof card includes safety tips and illustrated water exercises.

Alternative Therapies & Supplements for OA

BOOKS

The Arthritis Foundation's Guide to Alternative Therapies
This book contains research and advice on nearly 90 different alternative therapies for arthritis, from acupuncture to yoga. You'll also learn where to find a qualified practitioner, what to expect during an office visit, and how much a therapy may cost.

Support Groups

ArthritisSupport.com
www.arthritissupport.com
Lists local support groups by state, and has a research library, the latest news and information, a chat room, message boards, as well as advice for exercising with arthritis.

SupportPath.com
www.supportpath.com
Includes message boards and lists online support groups and upcoming Internet chats about various health topics, including arthritis.

Surgery

ORGANIZATIONS

**American Academy
of Orthopedic Surgeons**
6300 North River Road
Rosemont, Illinois 60018-4262
(800) 346-AAOS
www.aaos.org
Provides information on arthritis treatments, including surgery; website helps you locate orthopedic surgeons in your area.

BOOKS

**All You Need to Know About
Joint Surgery (from the Arthritis
Foundation)**
Has information on choosing the right surgeon and hospital, maximizing your time with your doctor, and addressing financial concerns regarding joint surgery.

Good Gadgets

Aids for Arthritis
35 Wakefield Drive
Medford, New Jersey 08055
(800) 654-0707
www.aidsforarthritis.com
Sells devices for your kitchen and bathroom, and products to help with everyday living, like grooming, car, and household items. Call or visit the website to request a catalog or place an order.

ADI Assistive Devices
4000 Brandi Court
Austin, Texas 78759
(800) 856-0889
www.geocel.com/adi/home.htm
Provides products to help with activities such as dressing, eating, cooking, and grooming. Call or visit the website to request a catalog.

Independent Living Products
10799 N. 90th Street
Scottsdale, Arizona 85260
(800) 377-8033
www.activeforever.com
Sells general assistive devices, plus aids for the workplace, office, home, or hobbies, as well as those for arthritis. Call or visit the website to request a catalog, or visit their retail store at the address above.

Clean Air Gardening
5200 Martel Avenue, #6Q
Dallas, Texas 75206
(888) 439-9101
www.cleanairgardening.com
Sells easy-to-use, ergonomic garden tools. Call or visit the website to request a catalog or order products.

OXO International
75 Ninth Avenue, 5th Floor
New York, New York 10011
(800) 545-4411
www.oxo.com
Specializes in easy-to-use products including Good Grips cleaning, cooking, and gardening tools with soft, flexible handles, or large grips designed to fit easily in the palm. Shop online or at retailers like Filene's, Linens 'n Things, Bloomingdales, Kohl's, Crate and Barrel, Macy's, JC Penney, and Bed Bath & Beyond.

Integrative Medicine Resources

Dr. Andrew Weil's Self Healing
The monthly health newsletter from Andrew Weil, MD. Call (800) 523-3296 for subscription information, or visit www.drweilselfhealing.com.

www.drweil.com
Dr. Andrew Weil's website for optimal health and wellness contains a new question and answer every weekday and a Vitamin Advisor.

**National Center for Complementary
and Alternative Medicine:
NCCAM Clearinghouse**
PO Box 7923
Gaithersburg, Maryland 20898
(888) 644-6226
http://nccam.nih.gov/
A branch of the US National Institutes of Health, NCAAM supports research on complementary and alternative medicine (CAM), trains researchers in CAM, and offers information on a variety of CAM therapies to the public. They can also provide specific information on osteoarthritis clinical trials and studies.

Selected References

Below, you'll find selected citations for studies, books, and other published material used in researching and writing this special report. In addition, *Self Healing* relied on information from organizations such as those mentioned in the Resource Guide (see page 74), interviews with physicians and other experts, and Dr. Weil's own experience in treating people with OA. The list that follows is a selective and by no means complete citation of references.

Chapter One: Understanding OA

American Family Physician, March 1, 2002; 65: 841–8. "Osteoarthritis: Diagnosis and Therapeutic Considerations."

Annals of Internal Medicine, October 17, 2000; 133(8): 635–46. "Osteoarthritis: New Insights. Part 1: The Disease and Its Risk Factors."

Annals of Internal Medicine, November 7, 2000; 133(9): 726–37. "Osteoarthritis: New Insights. Part 2: Treatment Approaches."

Archives of Internal Medicine, January 27, 2003; 163(2): 169–78. "Lack of efficacy of acetaminophen in treating symptomatic knee osteoarthritis: a randomized, double-blind, placebo-controlled comparison trial with diclofenac sodium."

Chemist & Druggist, October 26, 2002: 20–1. "The painful joint."

FDA Consumer, May–June 2000. "Arthritis: Timely Treatments for an Ageless Disease."

Integrative Medicine (Rakel, David; Saunders, 2003), p. 414–21

New York Times, July 30, 2002. "Arthritis: Your 'Reward' for Wear and Tear."

Postgraduate Medicine, October 1, 1999; 106(4): 127–34. "Getting Control of Osteoarthritis Pain."

Time, December 1, 2002. "The Age of Arthritis."

Q & A

Arthritis & Rheumatism, April 2002; 46(4): 946–52. "Genome Scan for Quality of Hand Osteoarthritis: The Framingham Study."

Link, February 2003. "The environment-health relationship: Osteoarthritis."

Rheumatology, August 2003; 42 (8): 955–8. "Osteoarthritis pain and weather."

The Journal of Rheumatology, February 2002; 29(2): 335–8. "Influence of weather conditions on rheumatic pain."

Chapter Two: Eating Well with OA

American Journal of Clinical Nutrition, March 1996; 63 (3 Supplement): 430S–432S. "Weight and osteoarthritis."

Annals of Internal Medicine, April 1, 1992; 116(7): 535–9. "Weight loss reduces the risk for symptomatic knee osteoarthritis in women. The Framingham Study."

Arthritis & Rheumatism, April 1996; 39(4): 648–56. "Do antioxidant micronutrients protect against the development and progression of knee osteoarthritis?"

Arthritis Foundation's Guide to Alternative Therapies, The (Horstman, Judith; Arthritis Foundation, 1999).

Journal of the American Geriatrics Society, September 2000; 48(9): 1062–72. "Exercise and weight loss in obese older adults with knee osteoarthritis: a preliminary study."

The Journal of Rheumatology, November 1998; 25(11): 2181–6. "Change in body fat, but not body weight or metabolic correlates of obesity, is related to symptomatic relief of obese patients with knee osteoarthritis after a weight control program."

Chapter Three: Keep Moving with OA

AARP: The Magazine, March–April 2003. "The Tao of Pain: Get Arthritis Relief by Mixing Eastern and Western Medicine."

Anchorage Daily News, June 3, 2003. "Movement eases pain of arthritis."

Arthritis & Rheumatism, November 1995; 38(11): 1541–6. "Guidelines for the Medical Management of Osteoarthritis. Part II. Osteoarthritis of the Knee."

Arthritis & Rheumatism, April 1997; 40(4): 728–33. "Risk factors for incident radiographic knee osteoarthritis in the elderly: The Framingham Study."

Journal of the American Geriatrics Society, December 2000; 48(12): 1553–9. "Effects of T'ai Chi training on function and quality of life indicators in older adults with osteoarthritis."

Strong Women and Men Beat Arthritis (Nelson, PhD, Miriam; Berkley Publishing Group, 2003).

The Journal of Rheumatology, December 1994; 21(12): 2341–3. "Evaluation of a yoga based regimen for treatment of osteoarthritis of the hands."

The Physician and Sportsmedicine, July 1997; 25(7). "Osteoarthritis: How to Make Exercise Part of Your Treatment Plan."

The Physician and Sportsmedicine, October 15, 1999; 27(11). "Exercises for Patients with Knee Osteo–arthritis."

The Physician and Sportsmedicine, October 2000; 28(10). "Exercise Benefits Patients with Osteoarthritis."

Chapter Four: Managing Pain with Mind–Body Measures

Arthritis Foundation's Guide to Alternative Therapies, The (Horstman, Judith; Arthritis Foundation, 1999).

Arthritis Week, May 25, 2003. "Depression strikes one in five black and Hispanic arthritics."

Image: The Journal of Nursing Scholarship, 1999; 33: 221–6. "Depression, social support, and quality of life in older adults with osteoarthritis."

Self Healing Guide to Alternative Therapies (Thorne Communications, 2002).

Chapter Five: Experimenting with Alternative Approaches

Acupuncture in Medicine, March 2002; 20(1): 19–21. "Effect of acupuncture on knee function in advanced osteo-arthritis of the knee: a prospective, non-randomised controlled study."

Agents Actions, July 1976; 6(4): 454–9. "An investigation of the therapeutic value of the 'copper bracelet'— dermal assimilation of copper in arthritic/rheumatoid conditions."

Alternative Therapies in Health and Medicine, March 2000; 6(2): 68–74, 77–80. "Randomized prospective double-blind placebo-controlled study of dextrose prolotherapy for knee osteoarthritis with or without ACL laxity."

Arthritis Foundation's Guide to Alternative Therapies, The (Horstman, Judith; Arthritis Foundation, 1999).

Journal of Family Practice, October 1998; 47(4): 271–7. "The effects of therapeutic touch on patients with osteoarthritis of the knee."

Self Healing Guide to Alternative Therapies (Thorne Communications, 2002).

The Physician and Sportsmedicine, August 2000; 28(7). "Are Your Patients Asking About Prolotherapy?"

Chapter Six: Choosing Supplements for OA

Alternative Medicine Review, February 2002. "Sulfur in human nutrition and applications in medicine."

American Family Physician, January 15, 2003. "Alternative therapies for traditional disease states: osteoarthritis."

Arthritis Foundation's Guide to Alternative Therapies, The (Horstman, Judith; Arthritis Foundation, 1999).

Journal of Family Practice, May 2002; 51: 425–30. "Safety and efficacy of S-adenosylmethionine (SAMe) for osteoarthritis: a meta-analysis."

University of California San Francisco news release, November 18, 1999: "UCSF named one of nine centers of National Institutes of Health study on treatment for knee osteoarthritis."

Chapter Seven:
Considering Joint Surgery and Other Treatments

American Family Physician, August 1, 2000; 62: 565–70, 572. "Intra-articular hyaluronic acid injections for knee osteoarthritis."

American Family Physician, June 1, 2002. "Hyaluronic acid cuts pain, improves knee osteoarthritis."

Journal of Family Practice, October 2002. "Arthroscopic surgery ineffective for osteoarthritis of the knee."

New England Journal of Medicine, July 11, 2002; 347(2): 81–8. "A controlled trial of arthroscopic surgery for osteoarthritis of the knee."

Strong Women and Men Beat Arthritis (Nelson, PhD, Miriam; Berkley Publishing Group, 2003).

Chapter Eight:
Living with OA

Agency for Health Care Policy and Research; Research in Action, Issue 4 (May 2002). "Managing Osteoarthritis: Helping the Elderly Maintain Function and Mobility."

Chapter Nine:
Exploring New Research Horizons

Arthritis & Rheumatism, October 2002; 46(10): 2549–52. "Uncoupling of type II collagen synthesis and degradation predicts progression of joint damage in patients with knee osteoarthritis."

Interview with John Klippel, MD, July 18, 2003.

Acknowledgements

Dr. Andrew Weil's Self Healing would like to thank the following people for their valuable assistance with this special report:

John Klippel, MD, current president and CEO and former medical director of the Arthritis Foundation

Adam Perlman, MD, MPH, director of integrative medicine at the Siegler Center for Integrative Medicine at St. Barnabas Healthcare System in Livingston, New Jersey, and author of Chapter 51: Osteoarthritis, *Integrative Medicine* (Saunders, 2003)

Suzanne Gauthier, associate vice president for health education, Arthritis Foundation, Massachusetts Chapter

Lorraine Hector, volunteer, Arthritis Foundation, Massachusetts Chapter

Oak Square YMCA, Adult Aquatics Department, Brighton, Massachusetts

Index